The Mystic Medicine Mandala Coloring Book

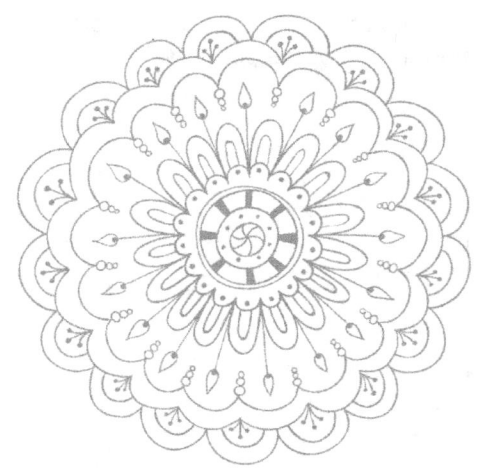

Dr. Keesha Ewers

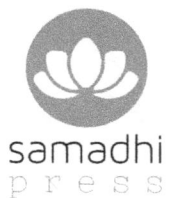

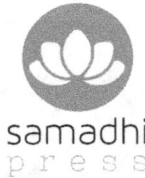

samadhi press

The Mystic Medicine Mandala Coloring Book
Copyright © Dr. Keesha Ewers, 2017

All rights reserved. This book or any portion thereof may not be reproduced or used in any manner whatsoever without the express written permission of the publisher.

First Printing: 2017
Printed in USA
Samadhi Press

Book Cover Design by Alex Gilman
Interior layout by Dani Hobbs

Dr. Keesha Ewers
410 Newport Way NW
Issaquah, WA 98027
(425) 391-3376
info@DrKeesha.com
www.DrKeesha.com

Ordering Information
Special discounts available on quantity purchases by corporations, associations, educators, and others. For details, contact publisher as above.

Booking, Press & Speaking Inquiries
www.DrKeesha.com/contact

This coloring book is not intended as a substitute for the medical advice of physicians. The reader should regularly consult a physician in matters relating to his/her health and particularly with respect to any symptoms that may require diagnosis or medical attention.

Dedication

"I found I could say things with color and shapes
that I couldn't say any other way—things I had no words for."
—Georgia O'Keeffe

For you, the mystic initiate, who is willing to plumb the depths of the mystery you have hidden from yourself. May you find joy and peace with the colors you paint your canvas with.

Introduction

"I sit with my mandala,
A sacred circle of beauty and life,
A map to the center of the universe,
A map to the center of me,
A design for healing heart, mind, body and spirit."

What is a Mandala?

Mandalas have existed from the beginning, from the beginning of time and the beginning of art. They are maps downloaded by mankind to explain where they fit in this universe of time and space. You see them all around you in every aspect of life. They are a circle. They represent life. They are a sacred symbol of the circle of life.

Mandala is a Sanskrit word meaning center or circle. It can be a simple geometric shape, or as you will notice in this book, a complex explosion of shapes and lines without beginning and without end. The act of coloring these sacred designs allows you to enlist your imaginative mind, your creative juices, and to tone the "rest-and-digest" part of your nervous system, giving the "fight-or-flight" portion some time off. This means these mandalas are a pathway to health and peace.

As you begin coloring your mandalas you may begin noticing more beautiful mandala designs in your environment. What about snowflakes, the sun's rays slanting through the forest in the early evening, the cells of your body? All of these fractal-like designs are representations of the grid of geometrical shapes and the grid of light that our very universe is made of.

Have you ever seen Tibetan monks painstakingly create their beautiful sand mandalas, representations of the layers of consciousness and spiritual planes? I work with my patients and students on the Medicine Wheel, a mandala similar to the mesas used in the Andes of Peru and the medicine wheels that are sacred to the Native American communities in our country. Mandalas are sacred, symbolic, and ceremonial; perfect for ritualizing the release of what no longer serves you and attracting to you what you want to have more of in your life.

As you pick up your coloring pencil, pen, or crayon and begin to add color to this book, do it with some intention. What would you like to release in your life that no longer serves you? What do you want to attract? Allow the mandalas to provide a sacred space for you to create the life you have always wanted to live, with intention. You are, after all, unlimited and unbounded powerful potential!

You can enlist the power of the mandala to:

- Deepen and focus your meditation.
- Bring balance to your heart, mind, body and spirit.
- Connect to God/dess.
- Spark your creativity.
- Enhance your self-awareness.
- Increase your ability forself-expression.
- Provide harmony, peace, calm and fun.

Relax, enjoy and be prepared to be transformed! Much love and many blessings,

Dr. Keesha

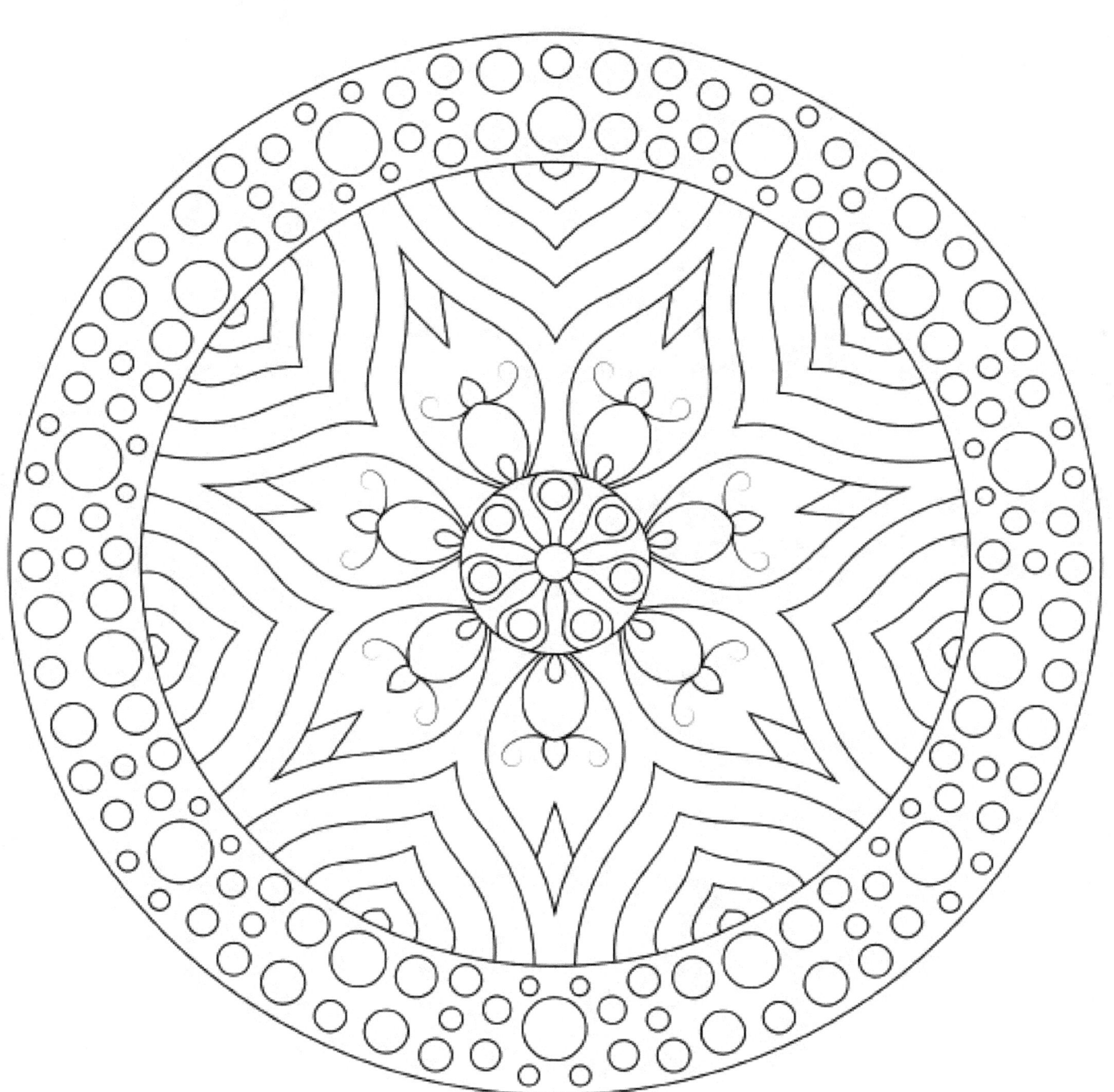

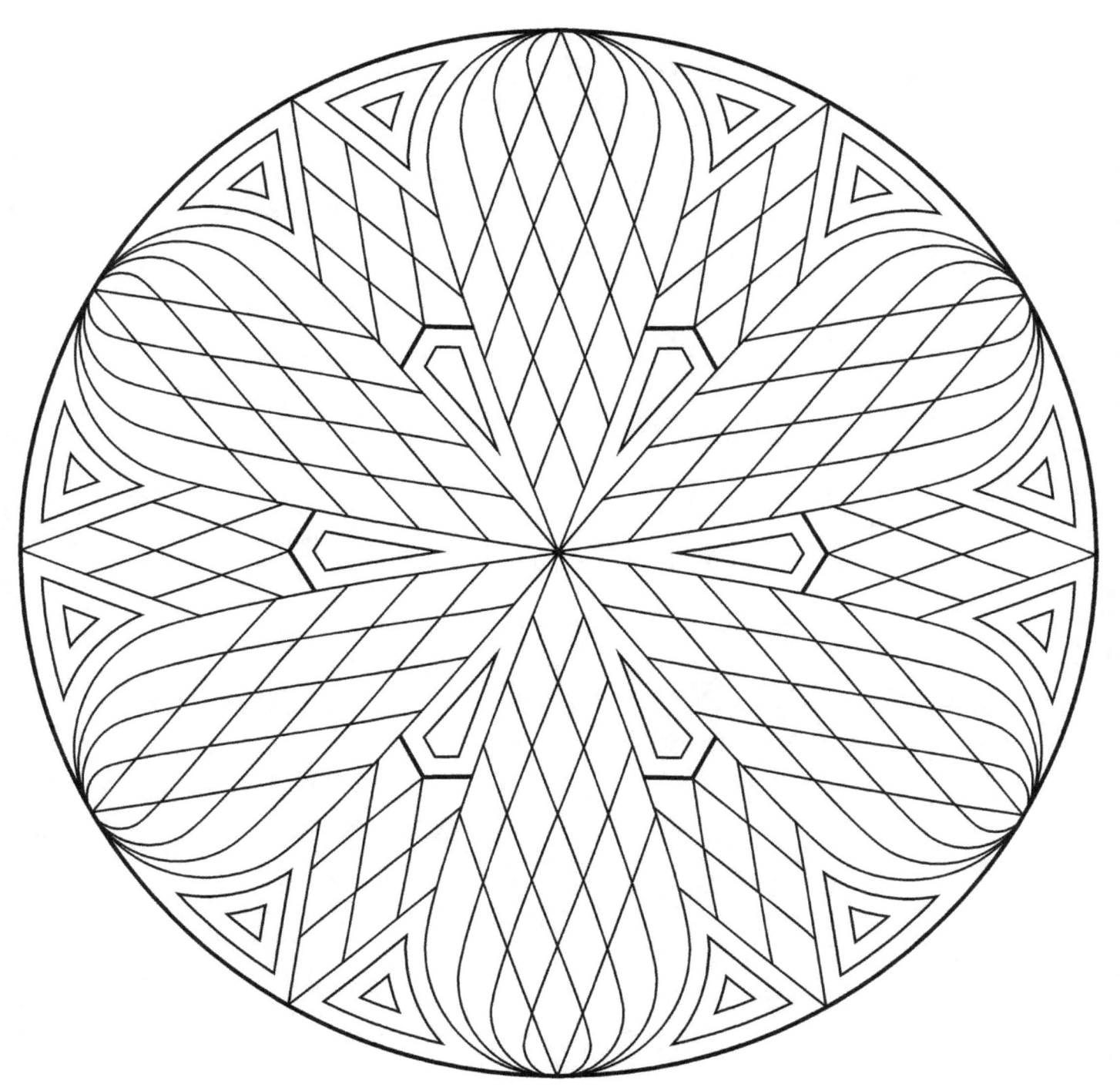

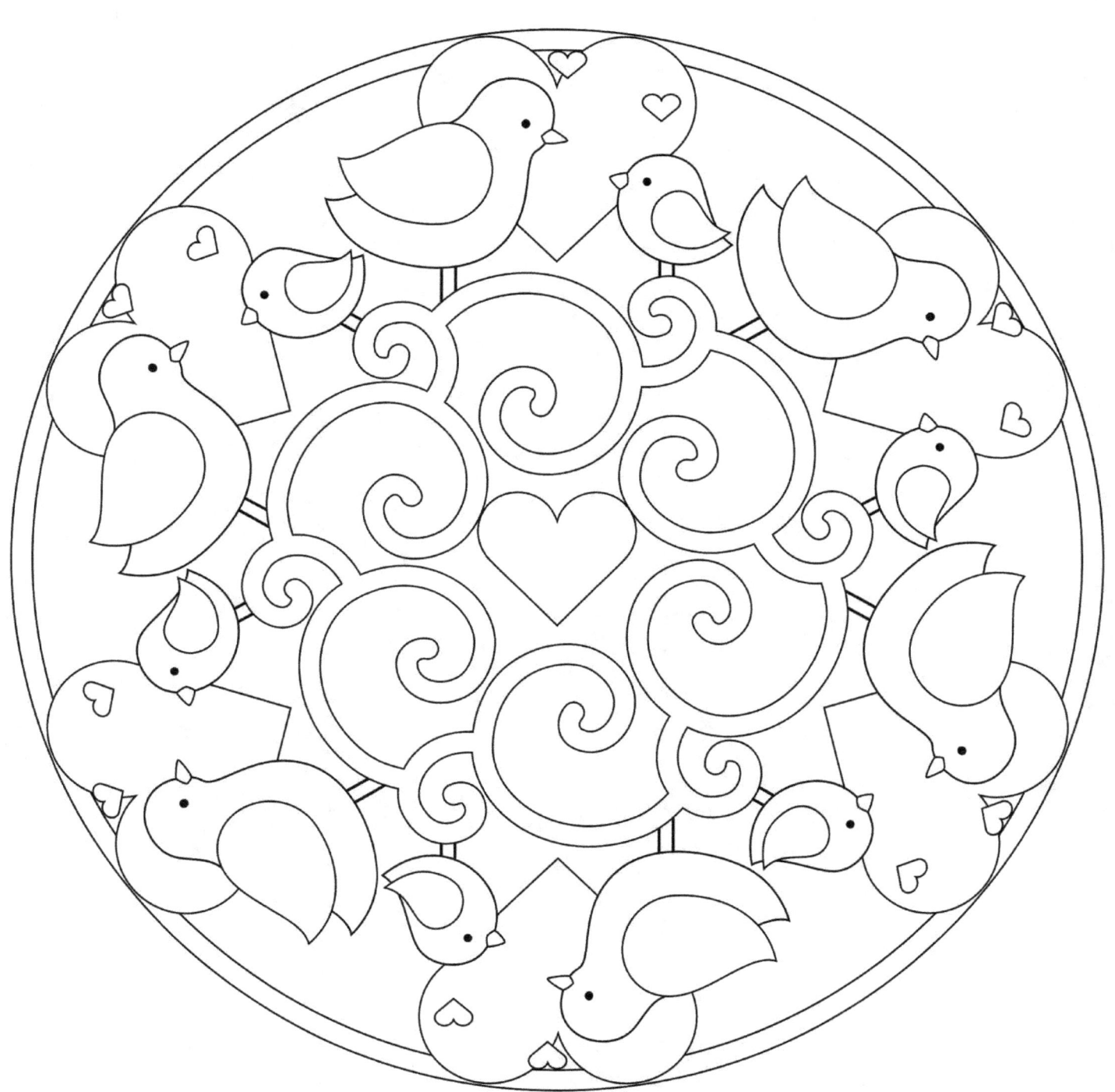

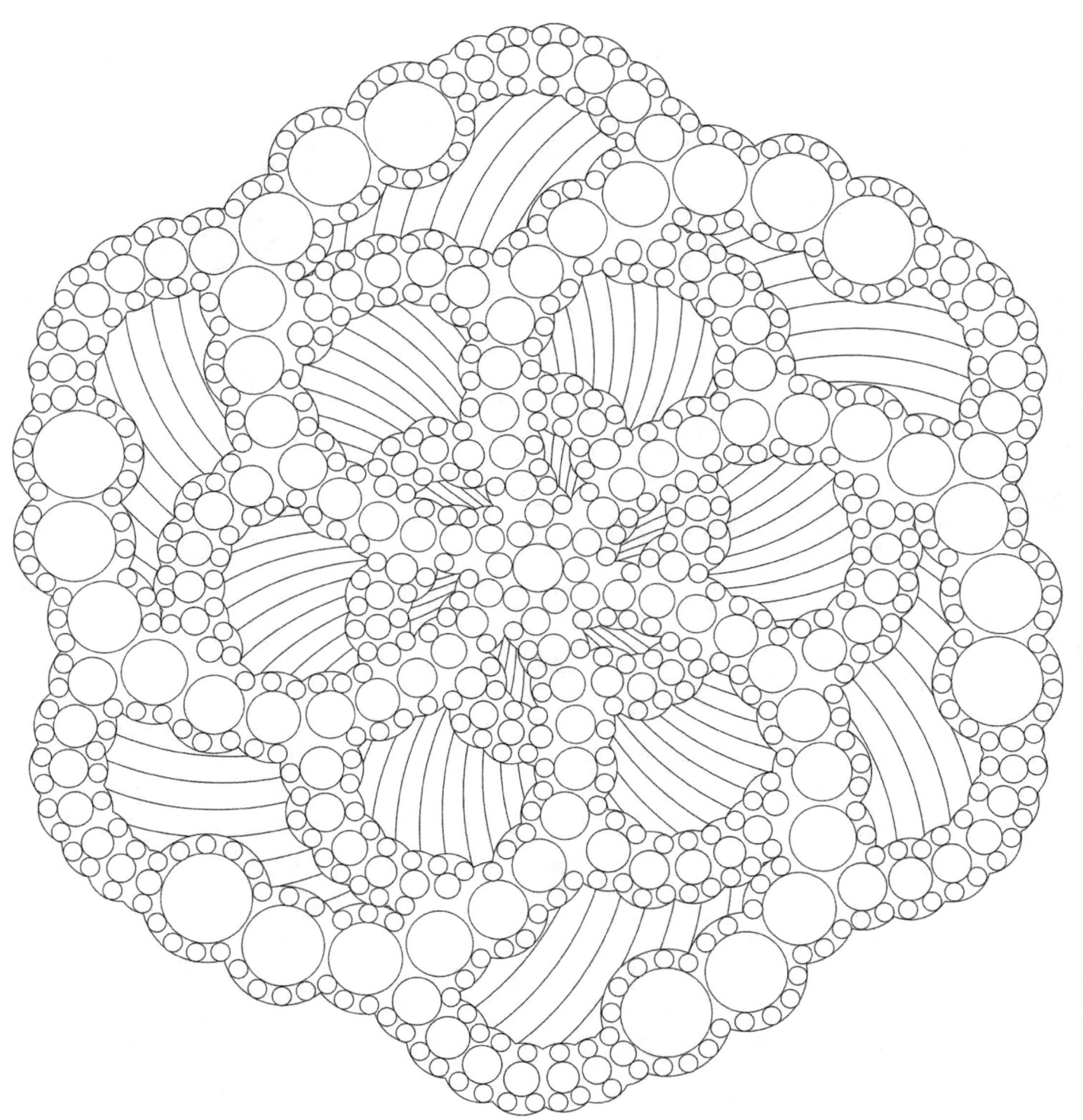

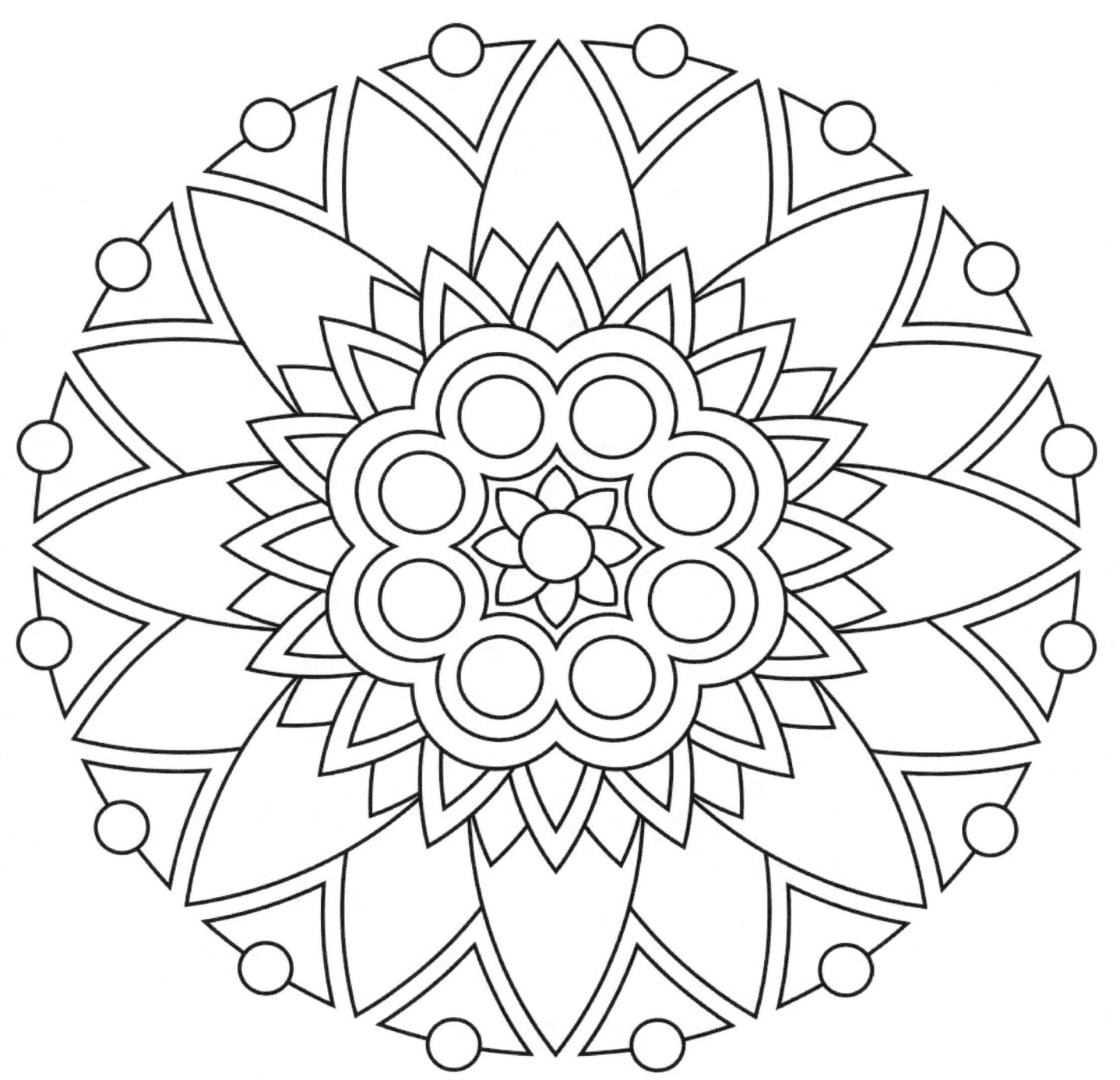

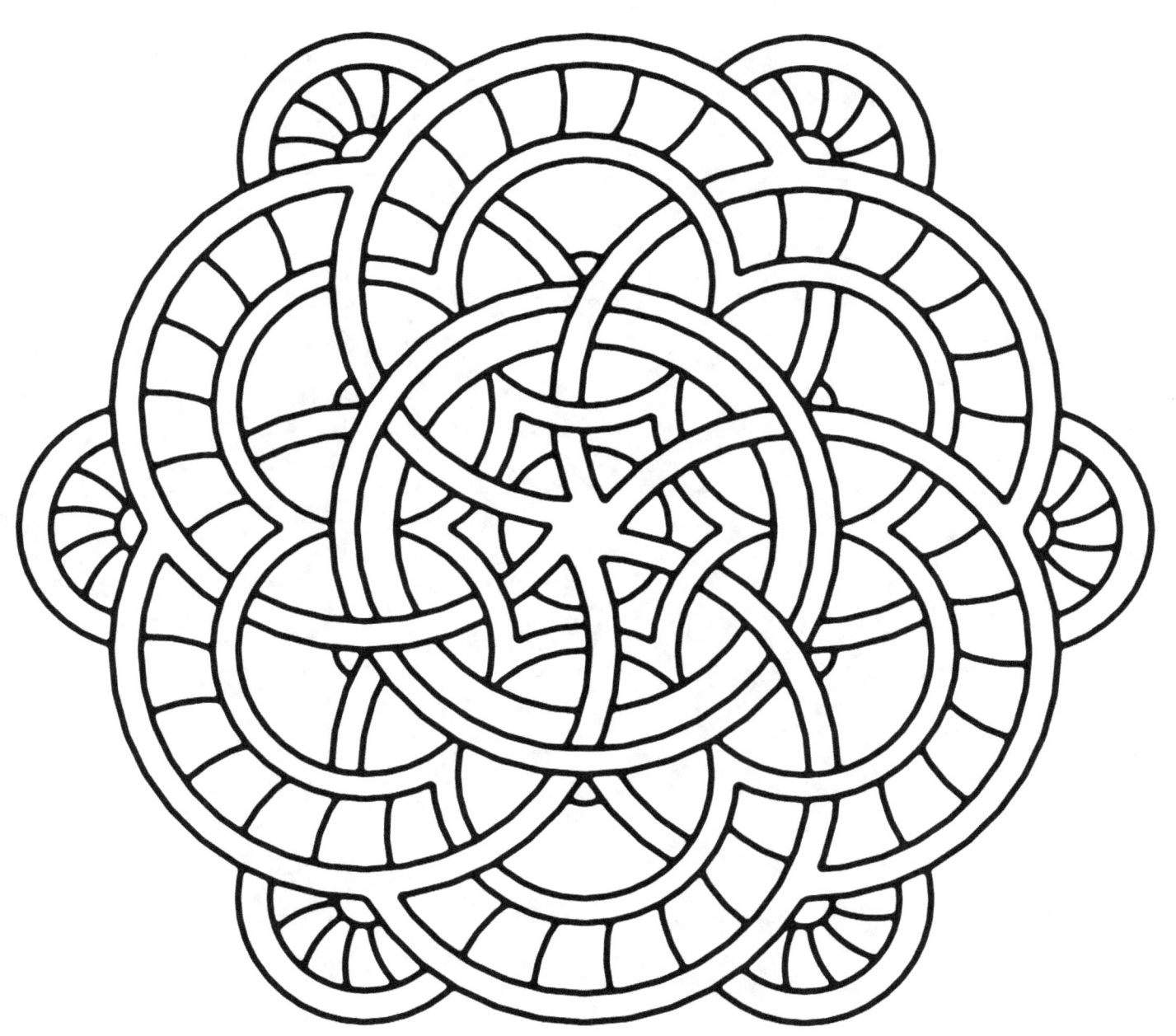

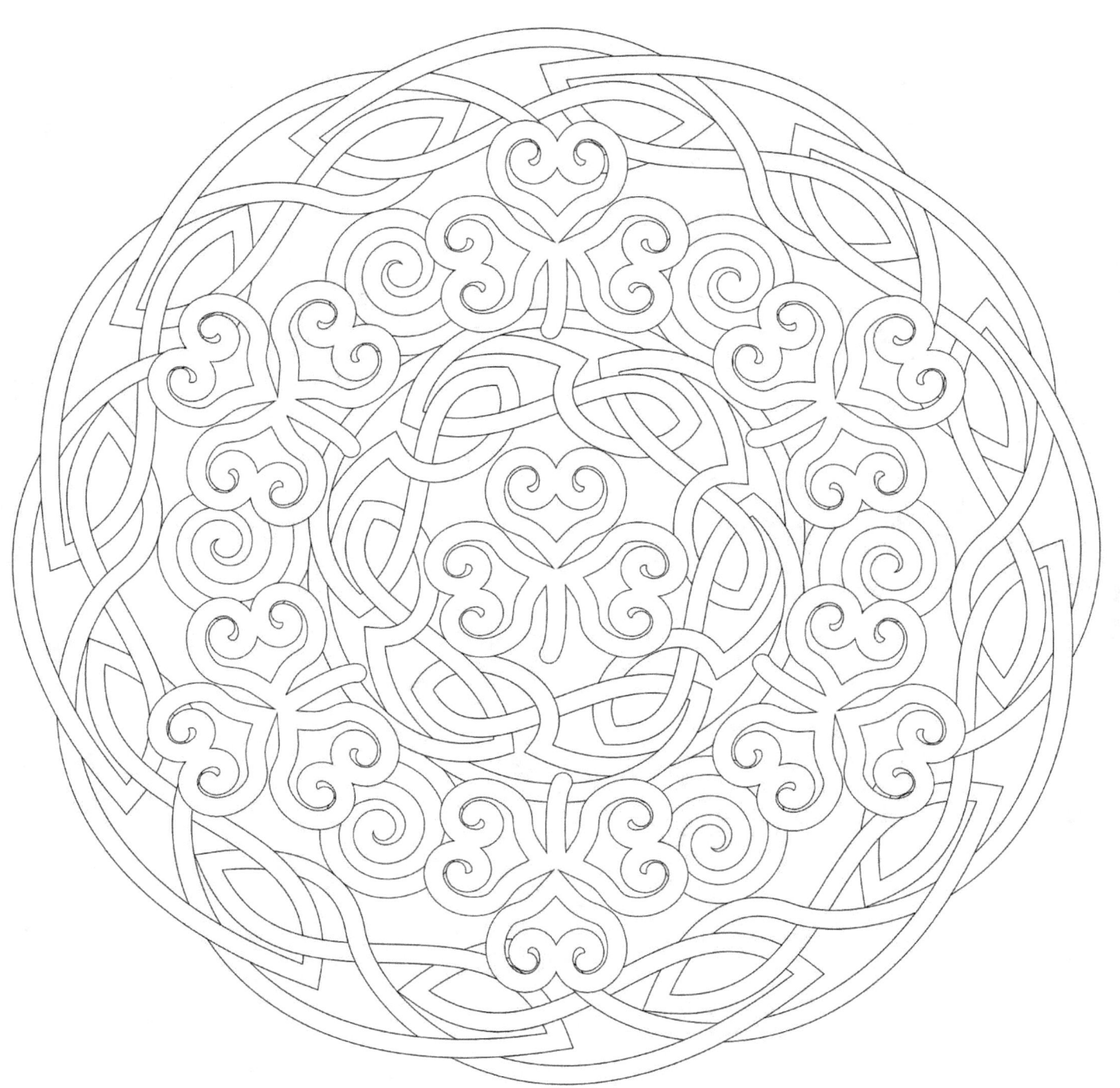

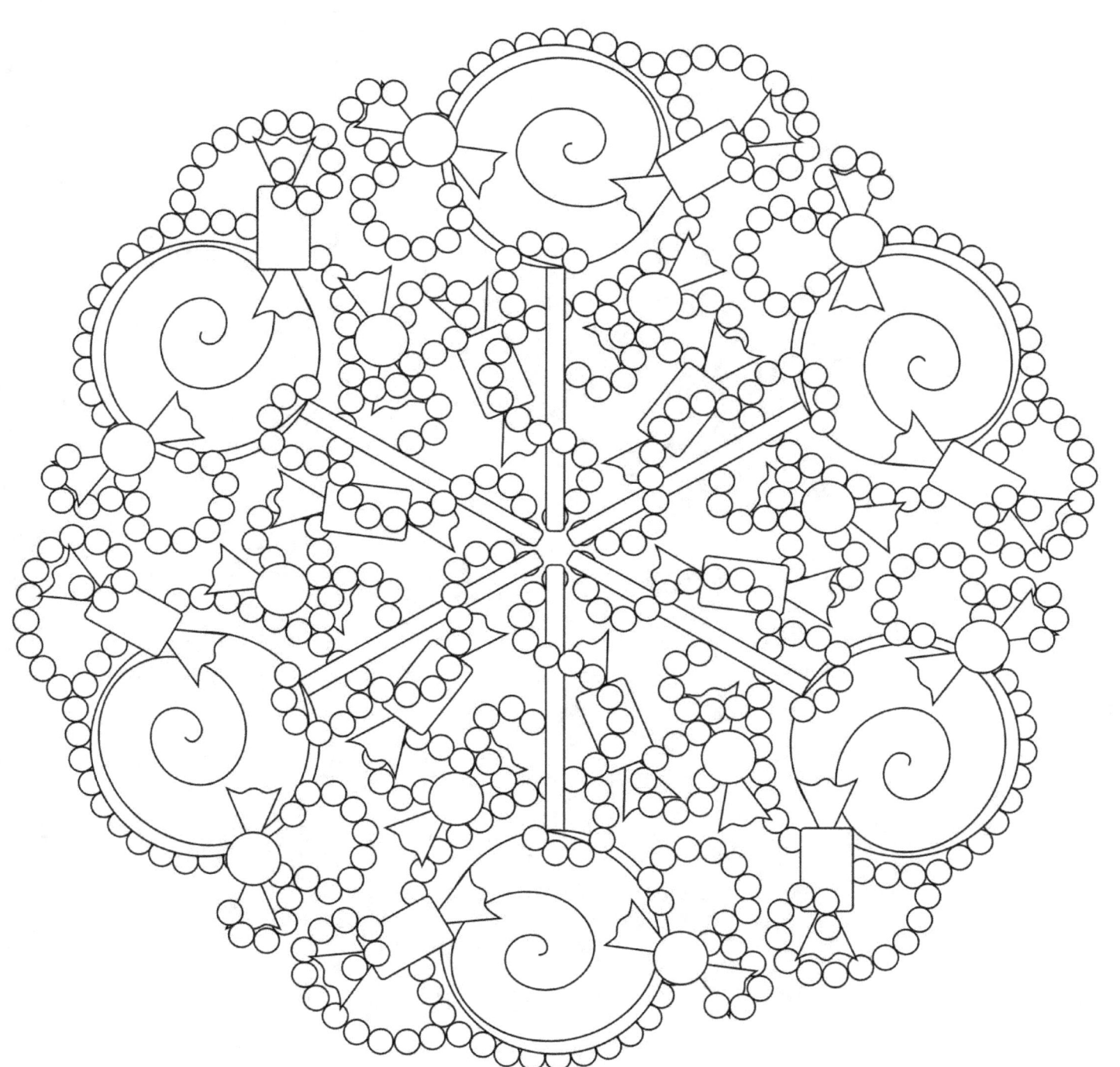

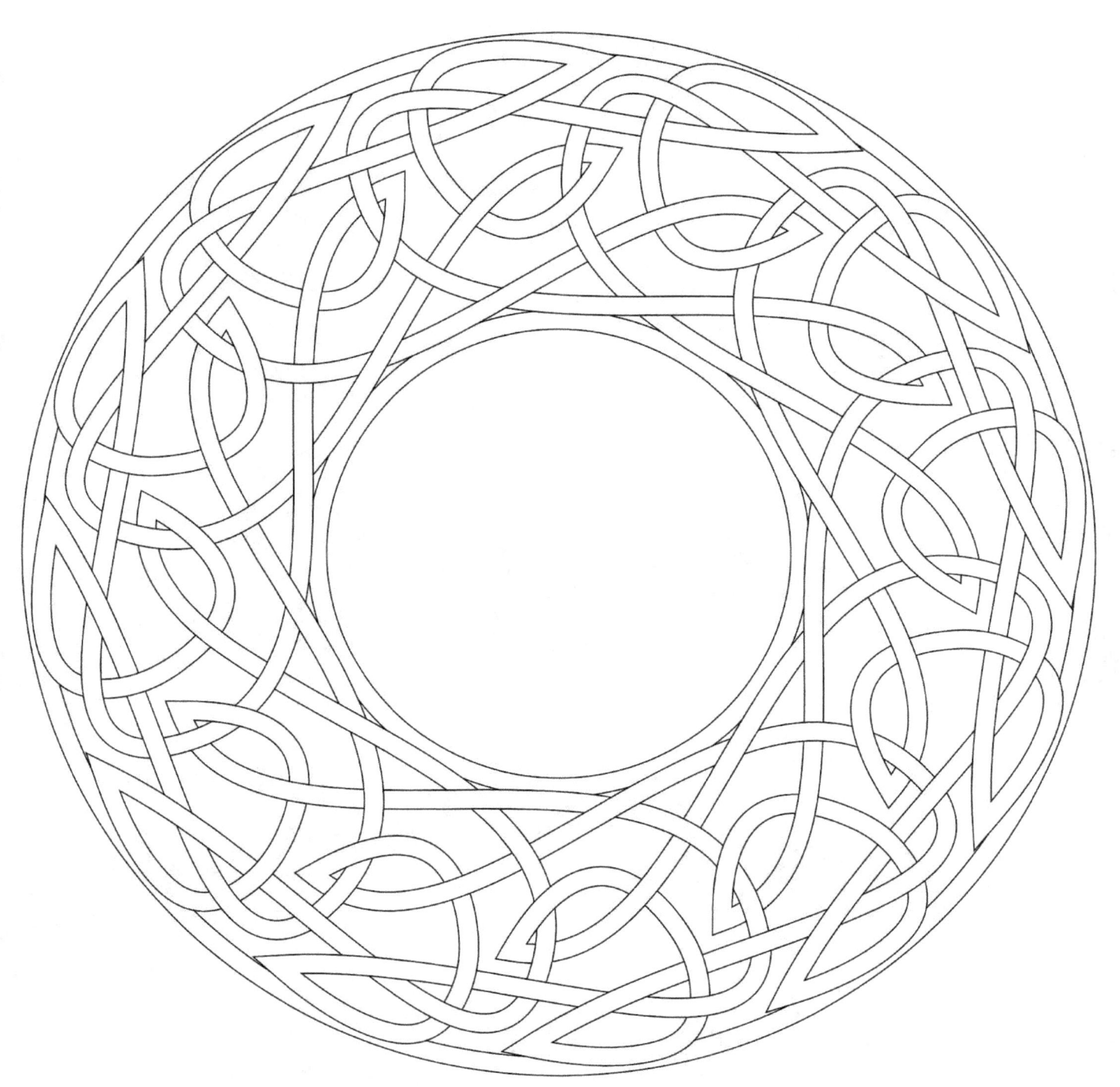

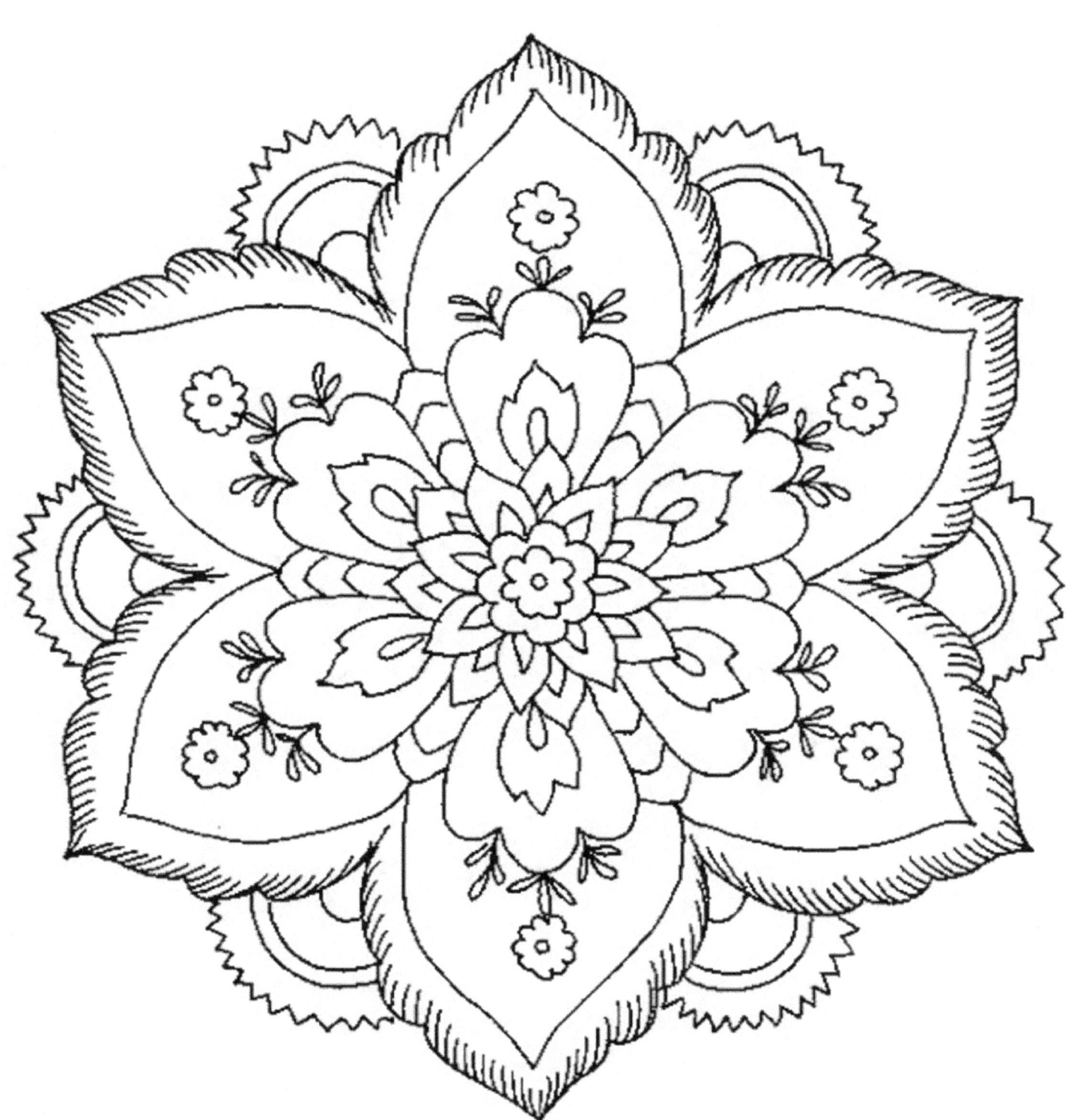

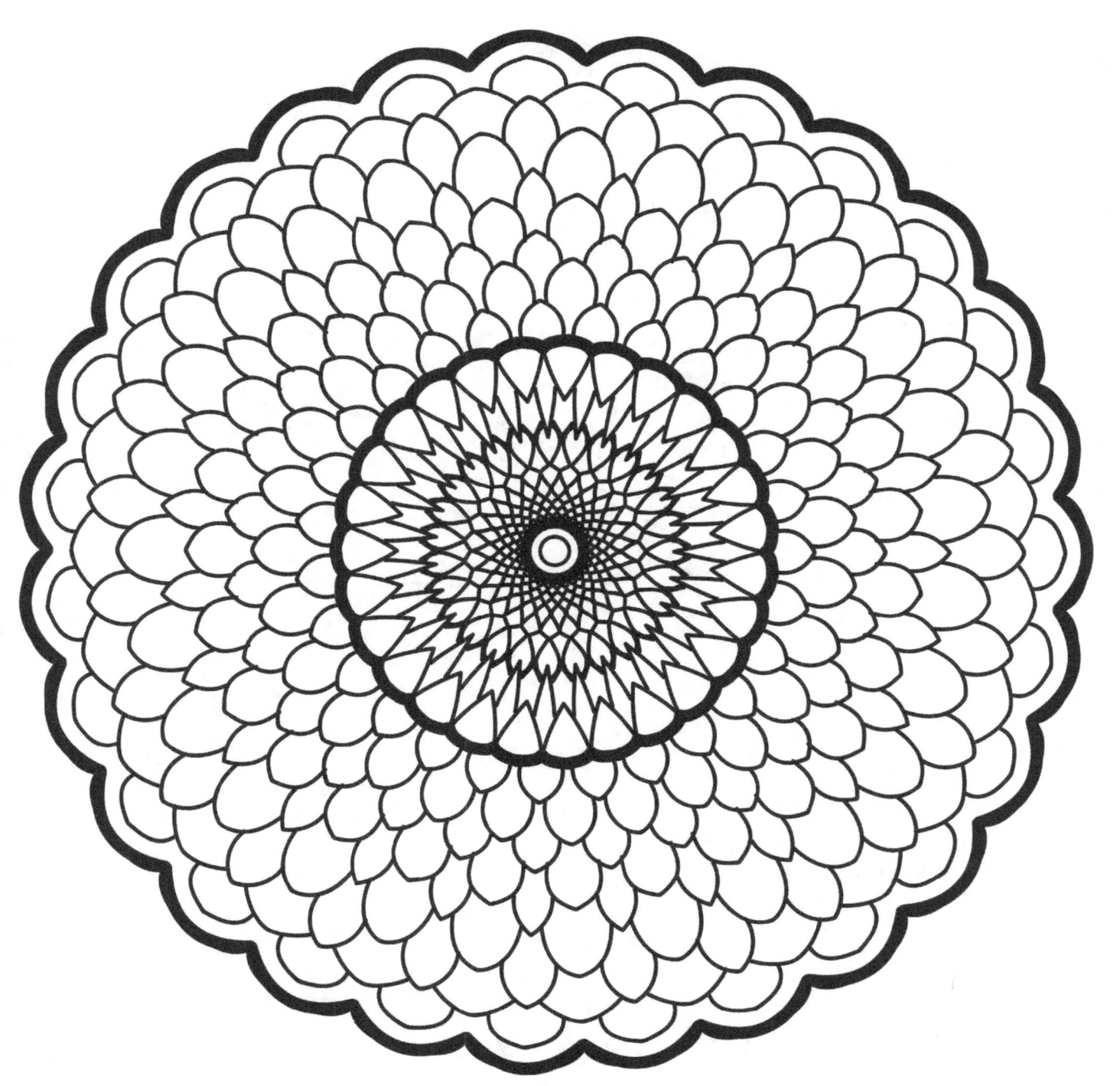

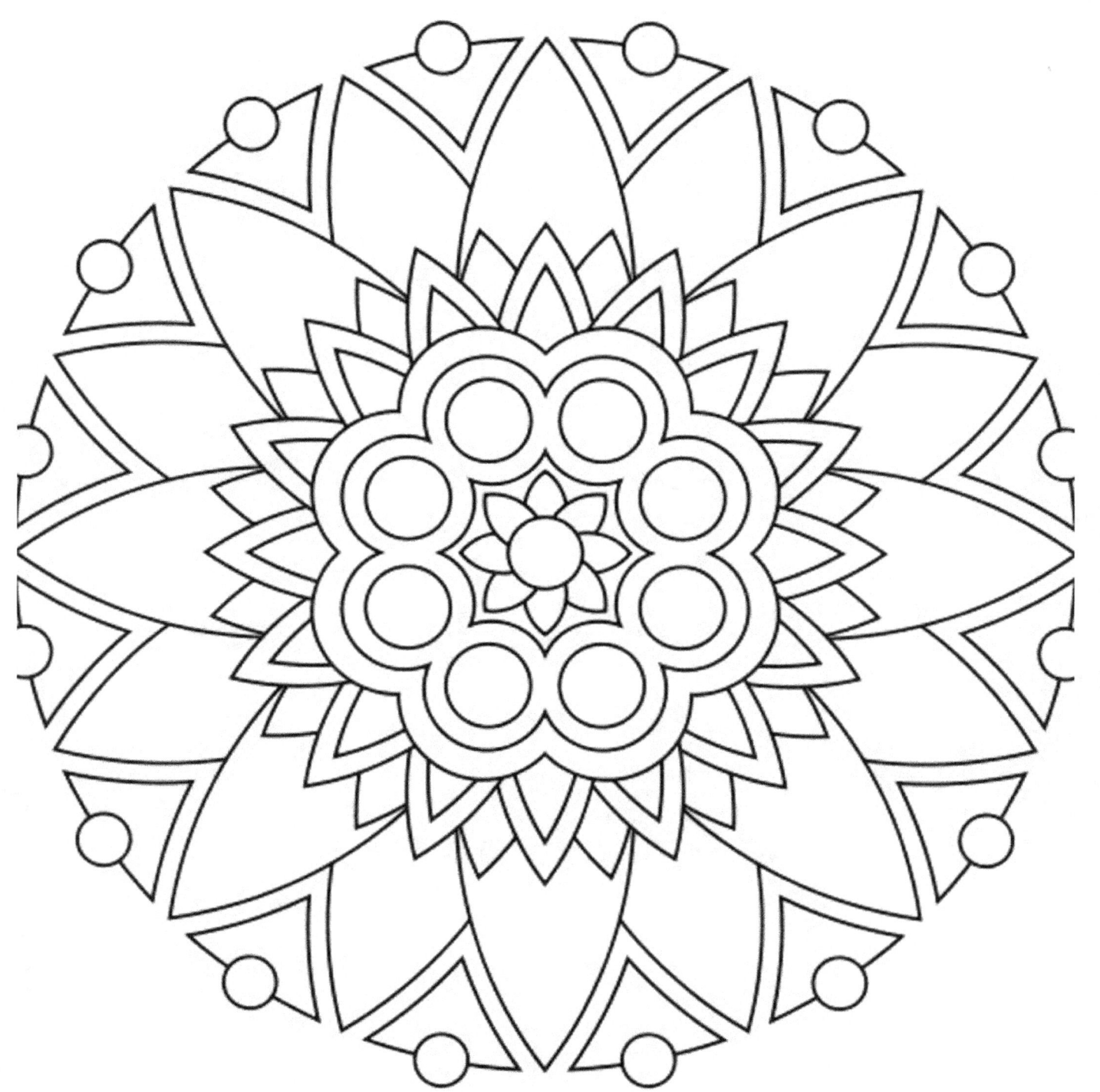

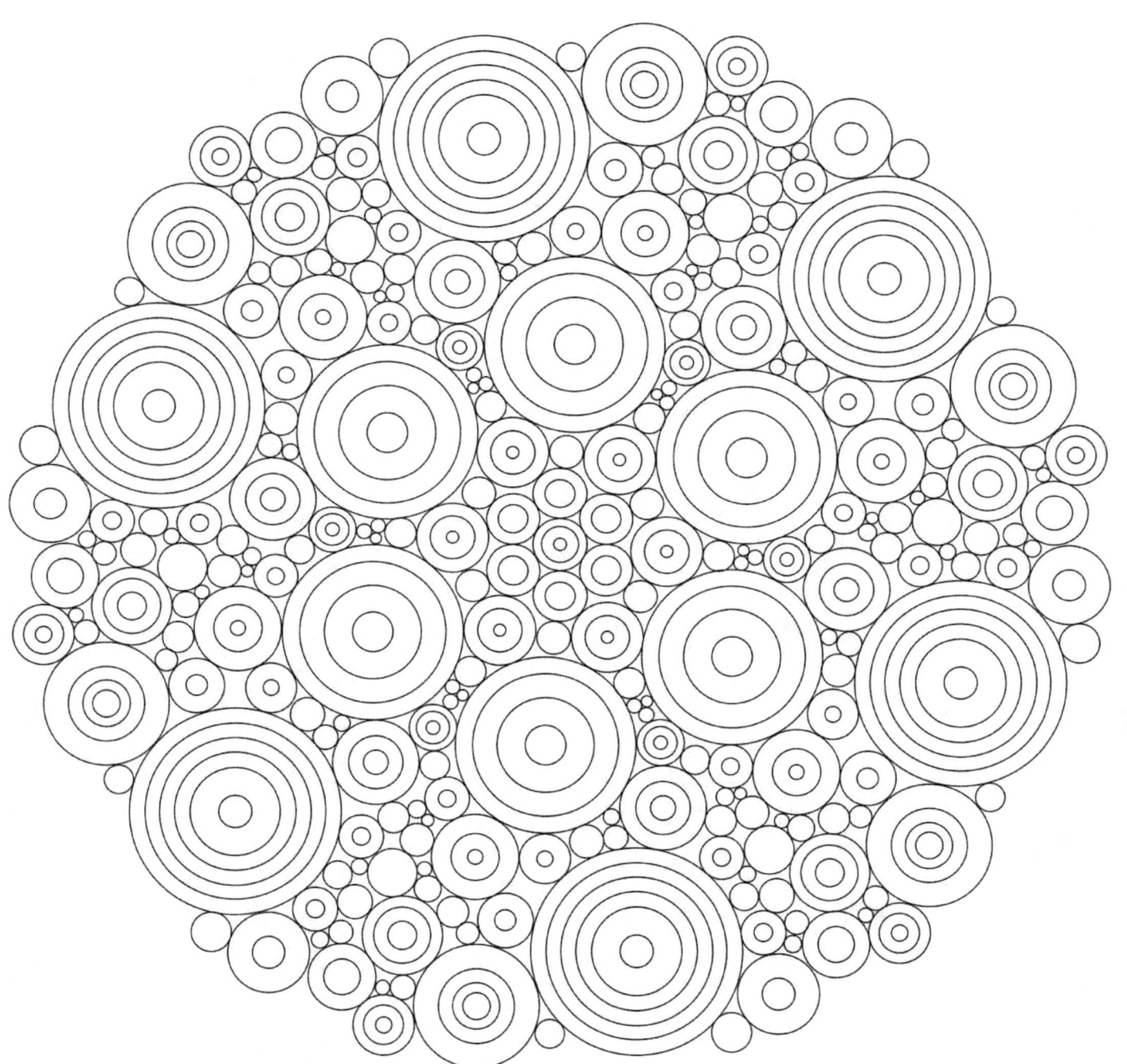

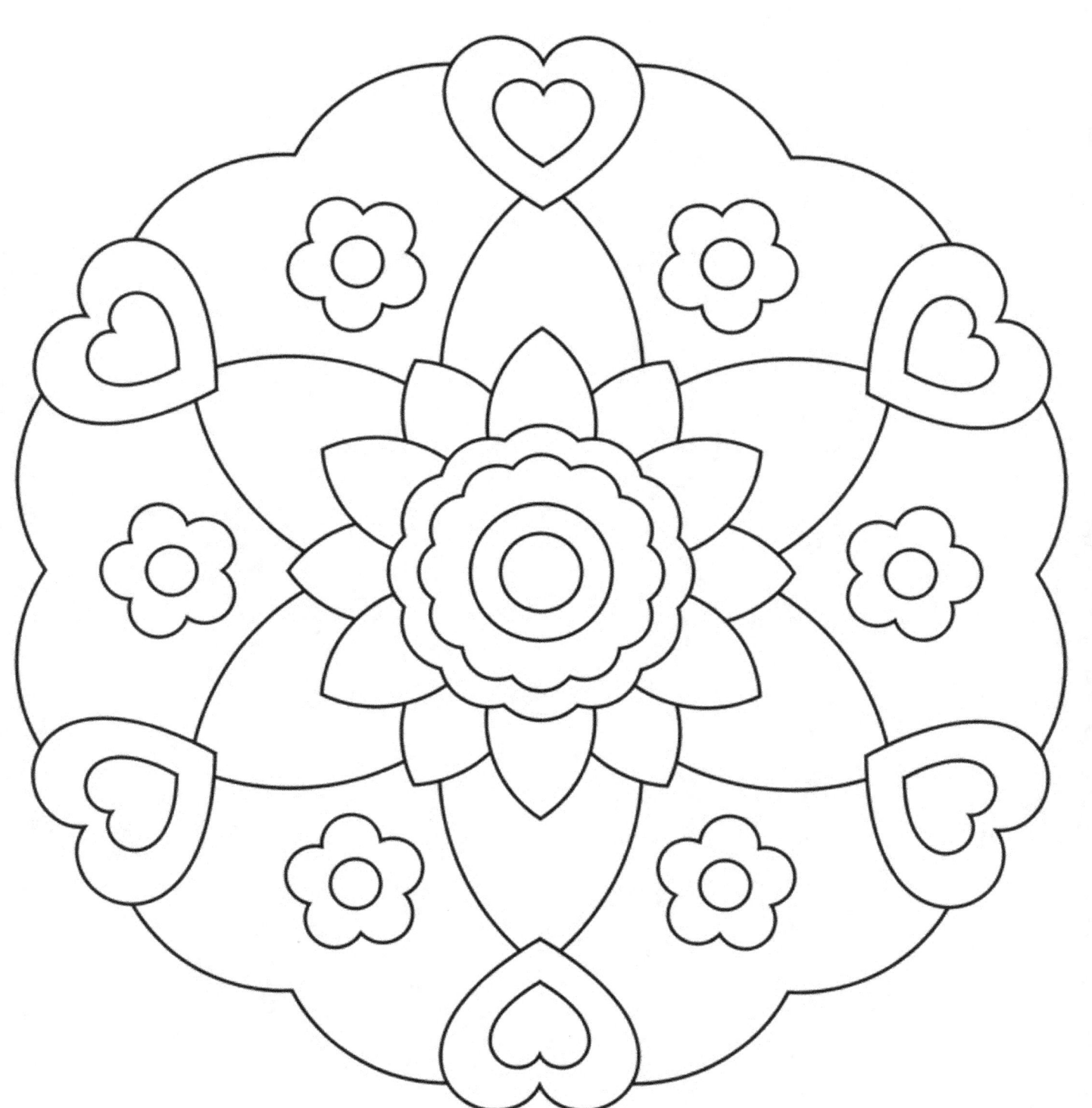

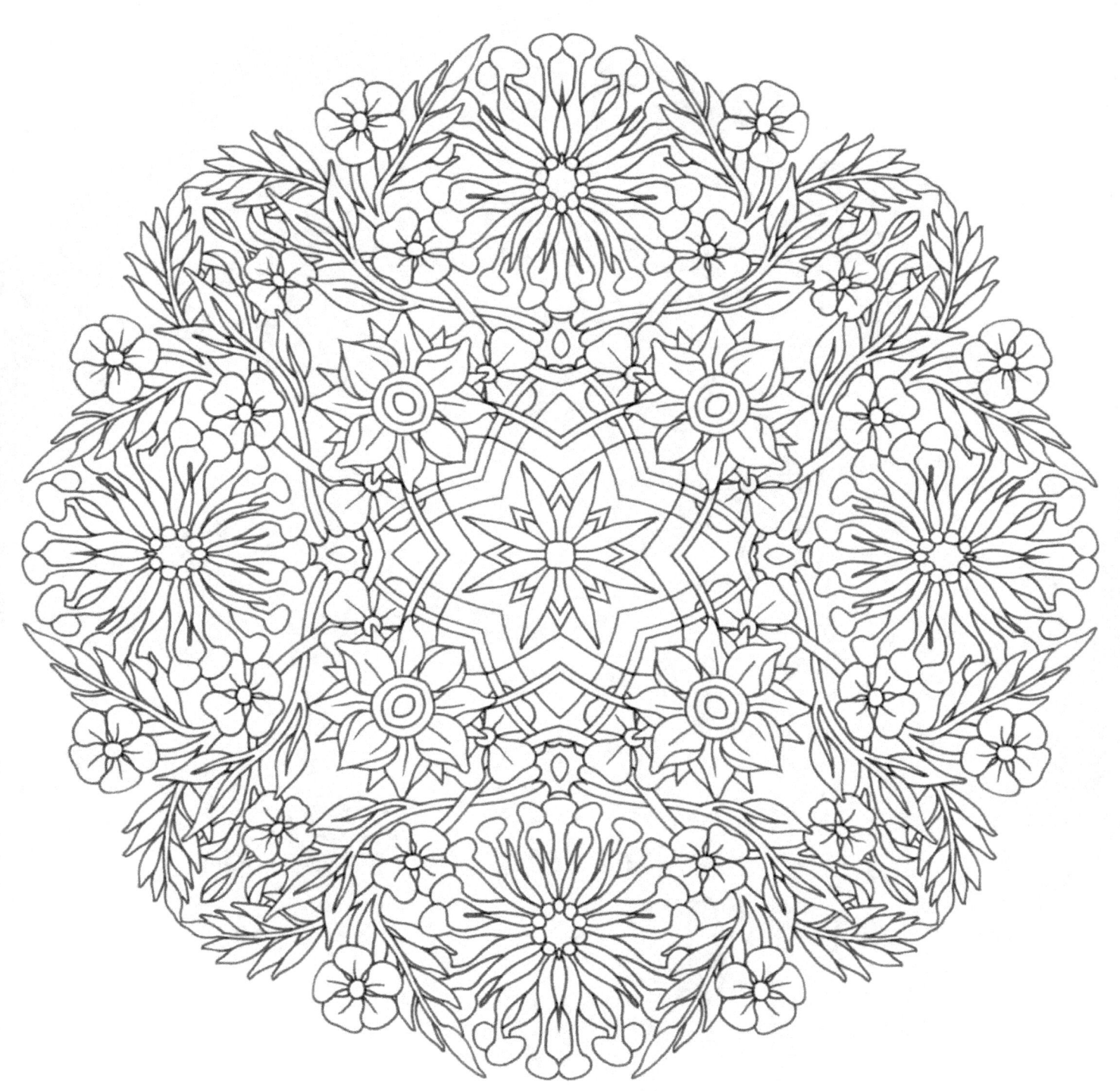

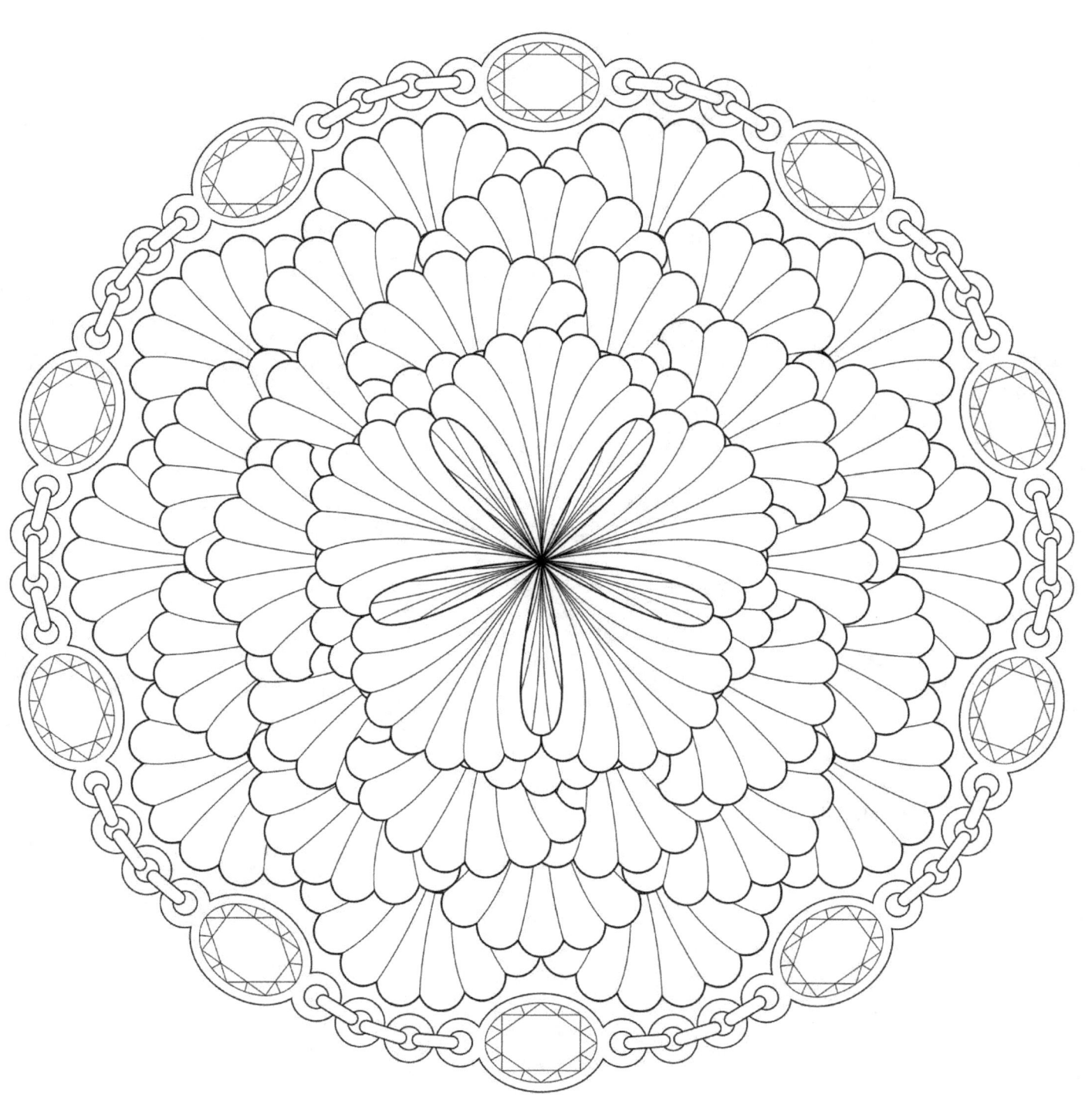

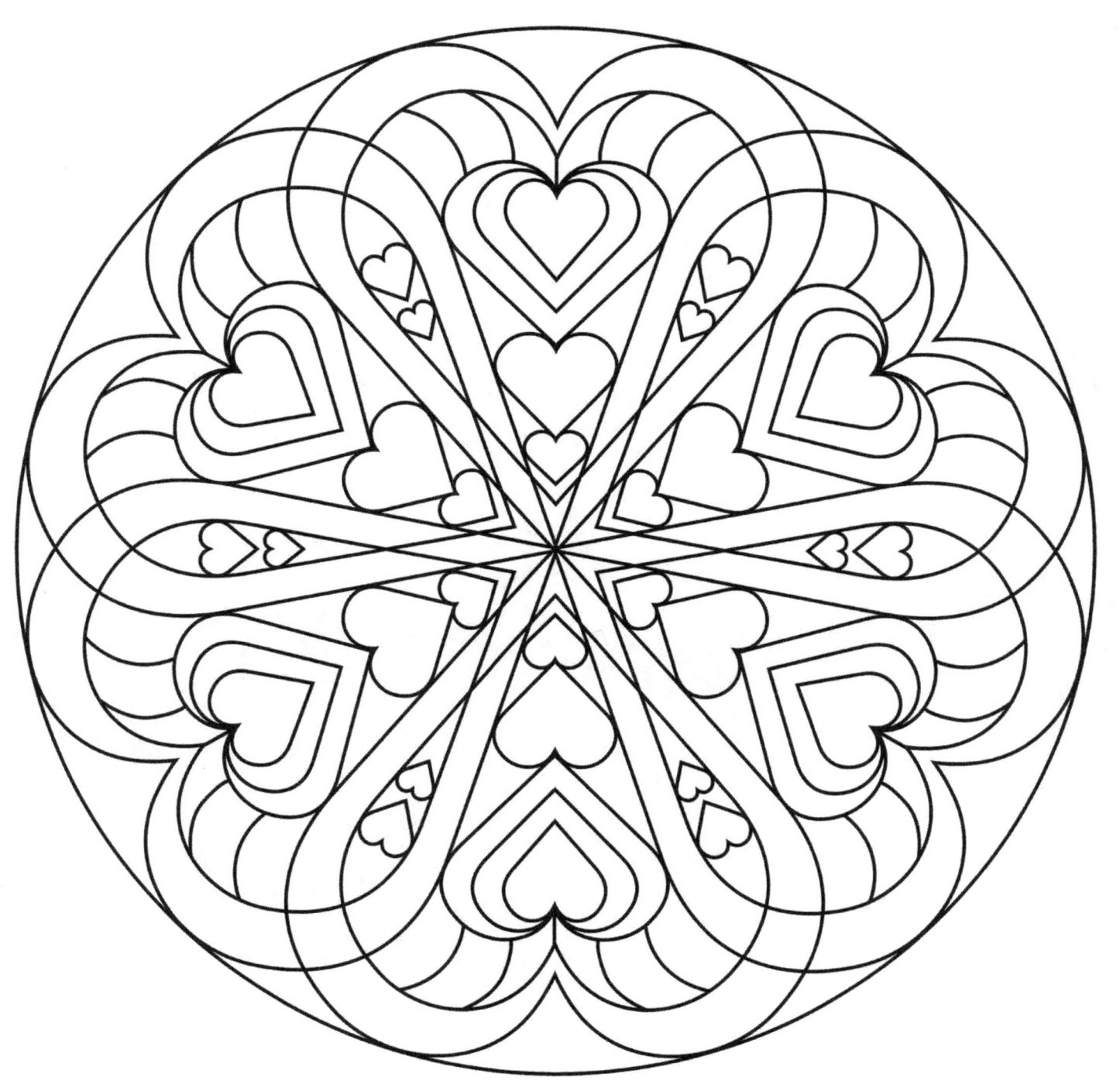

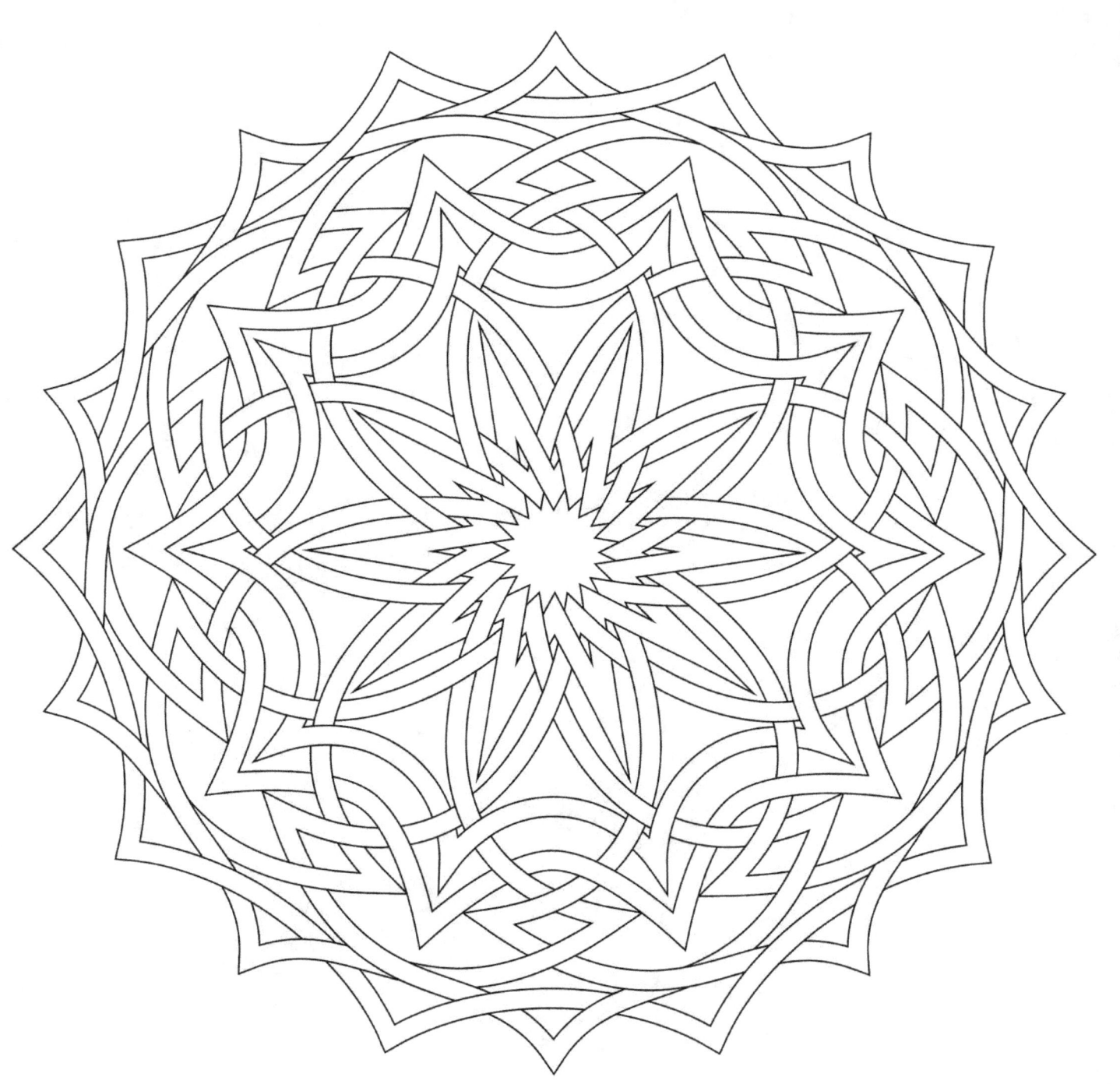

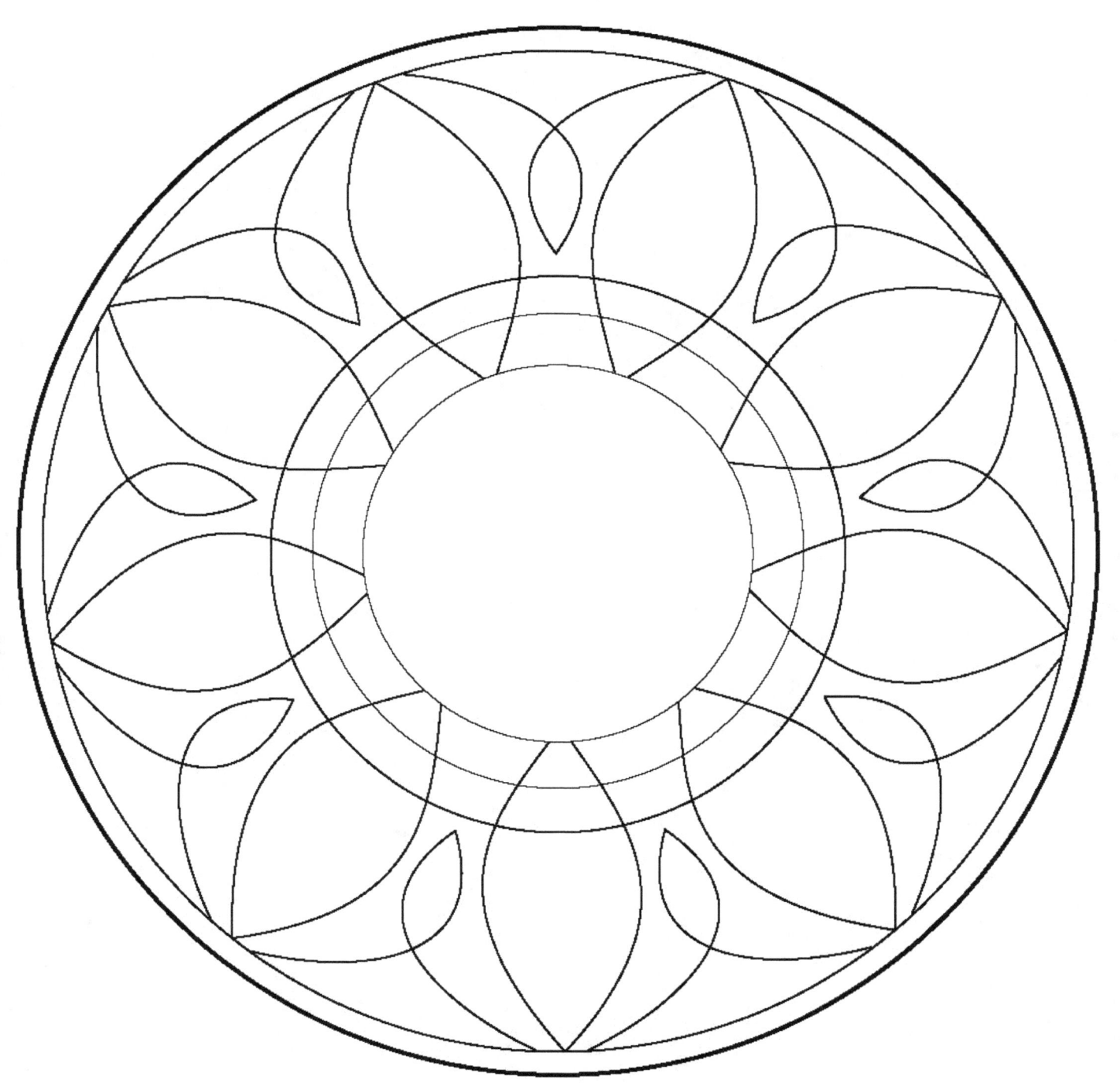

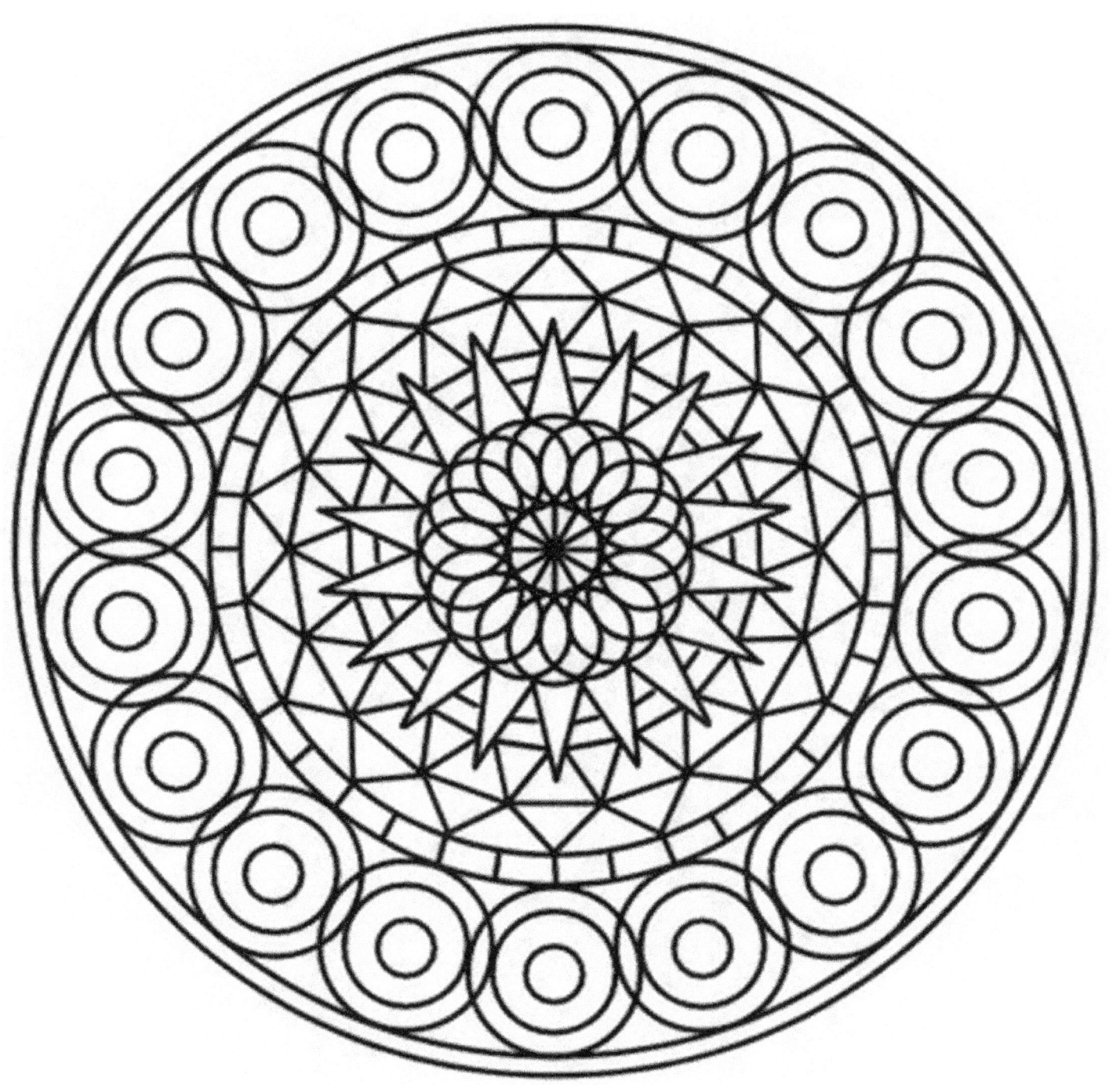

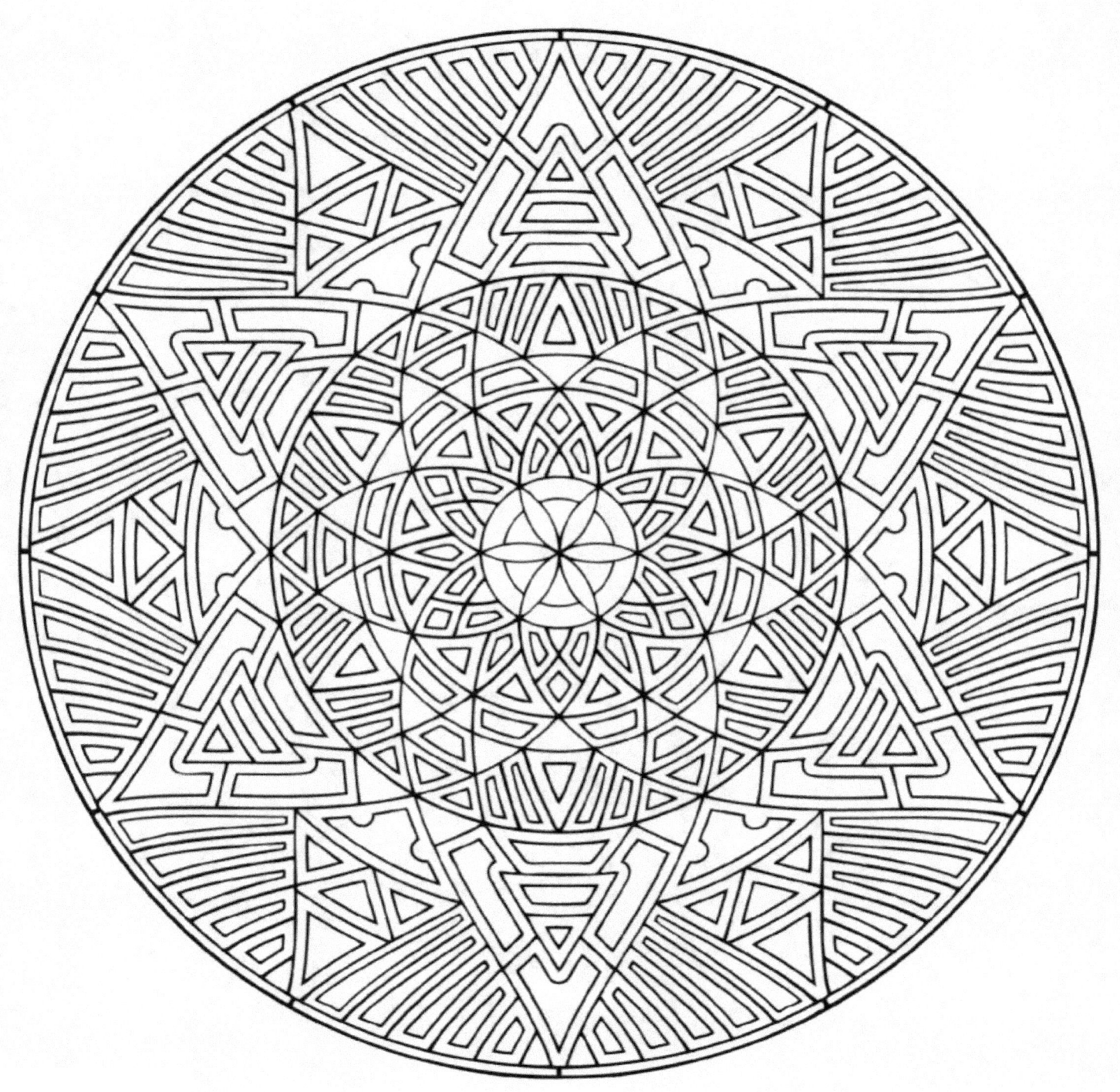

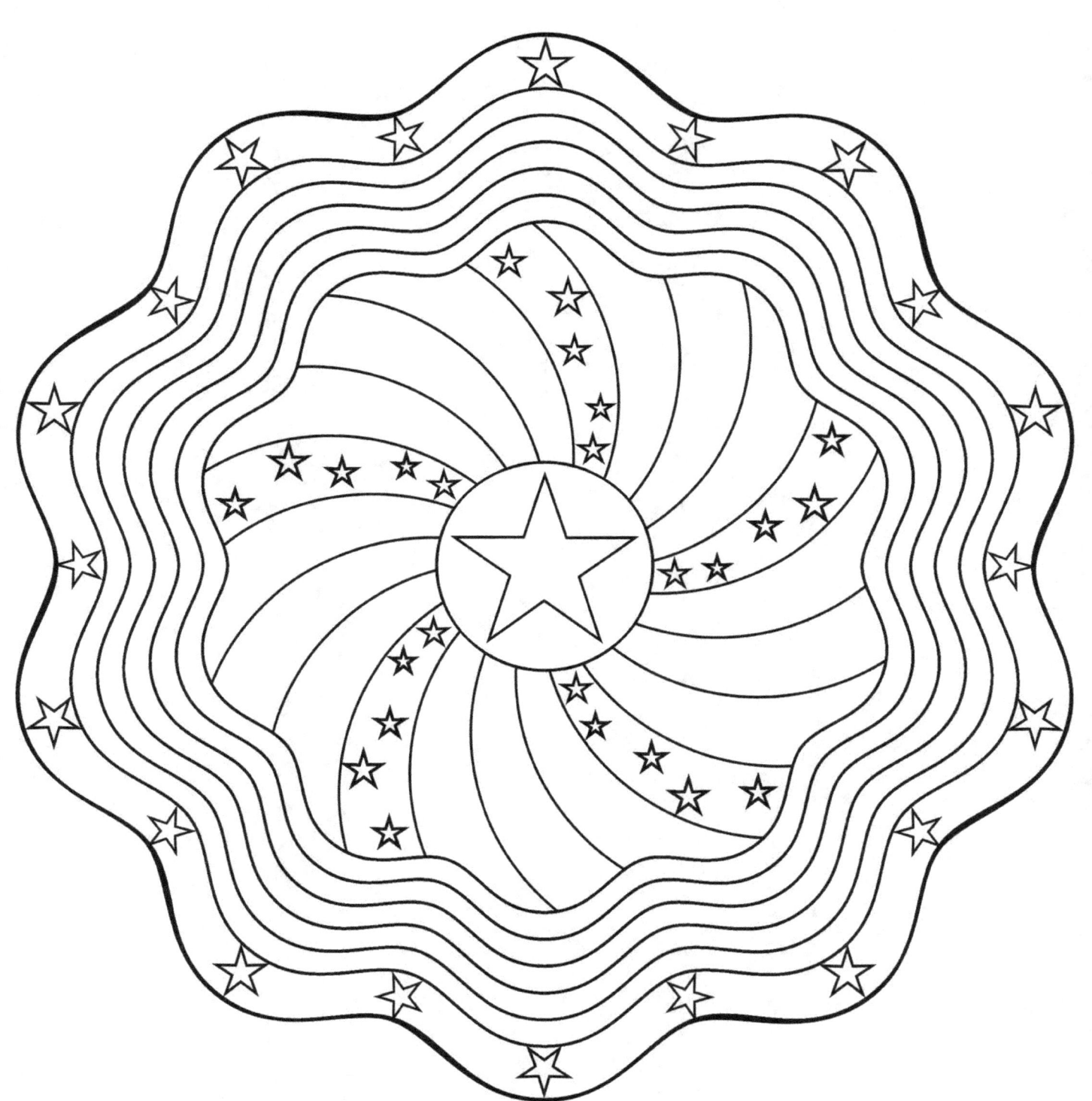

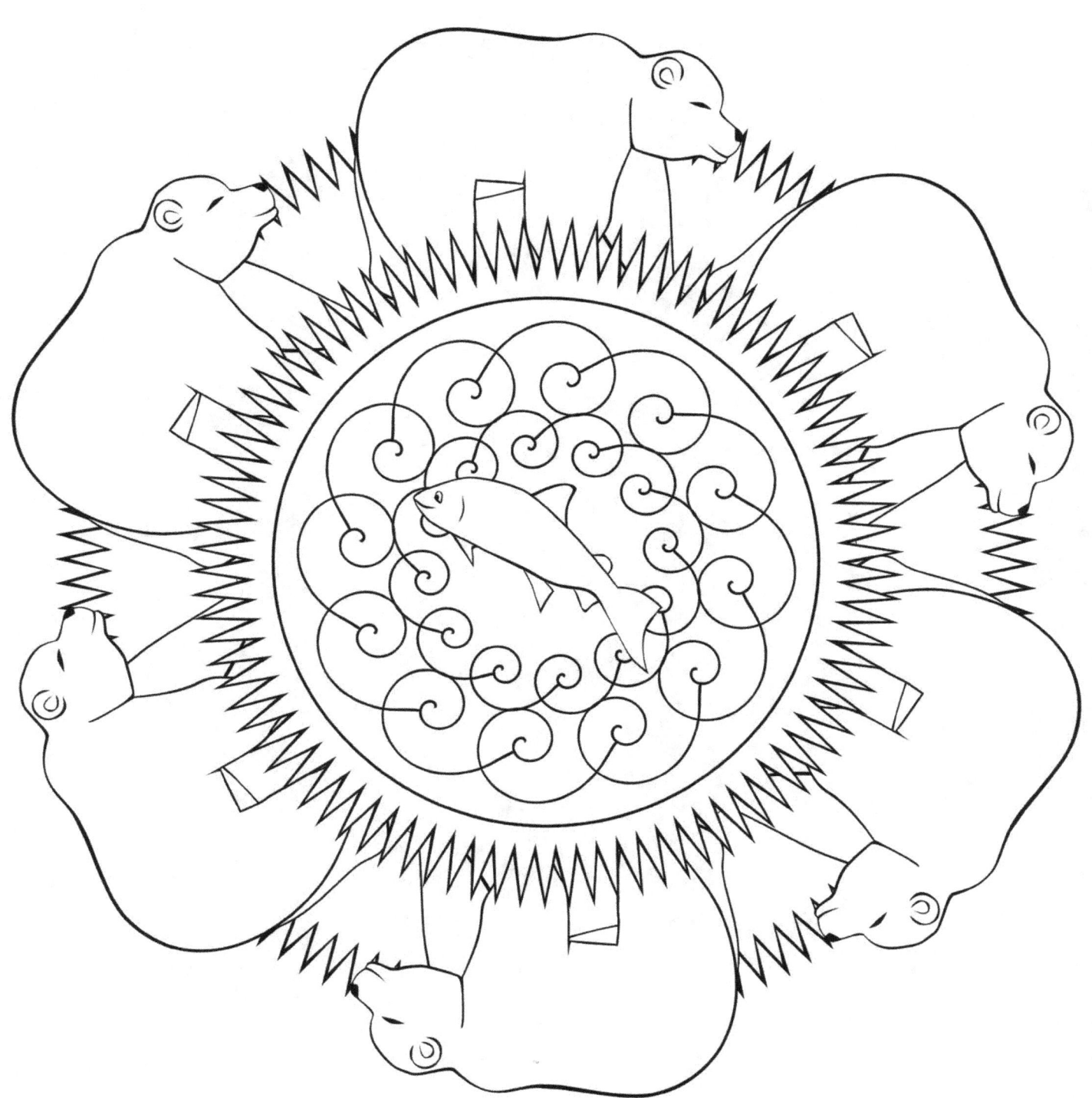

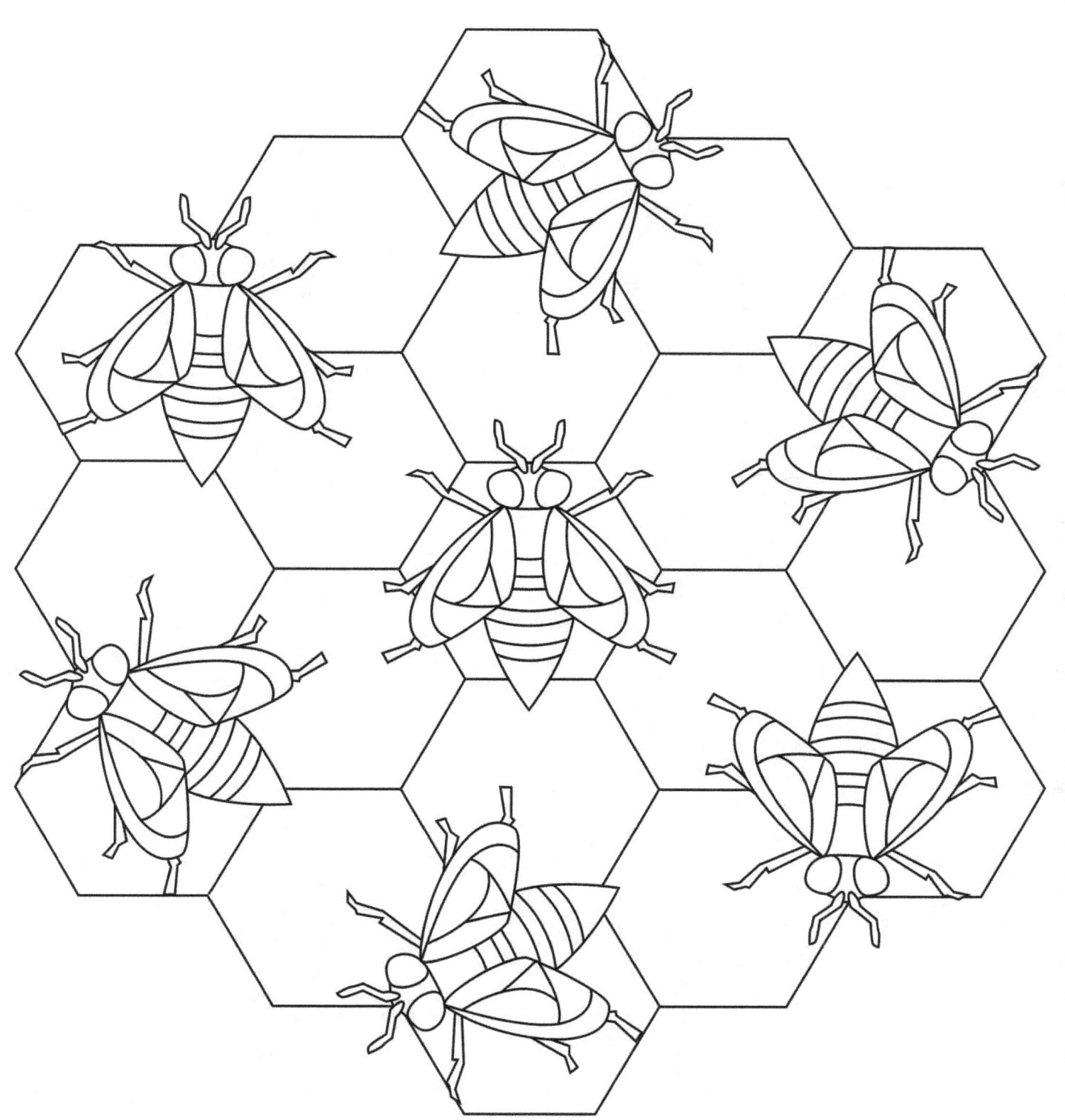

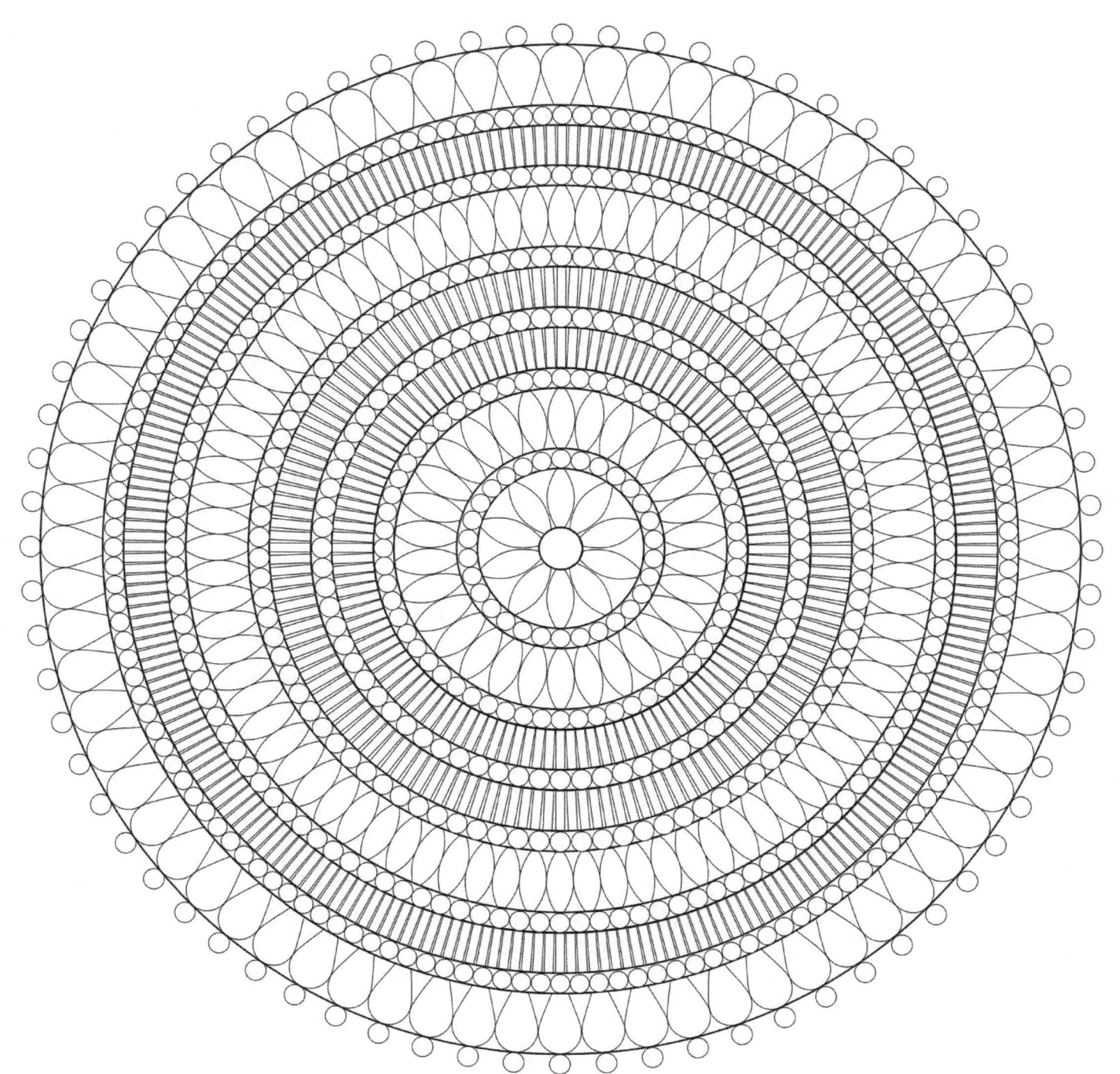

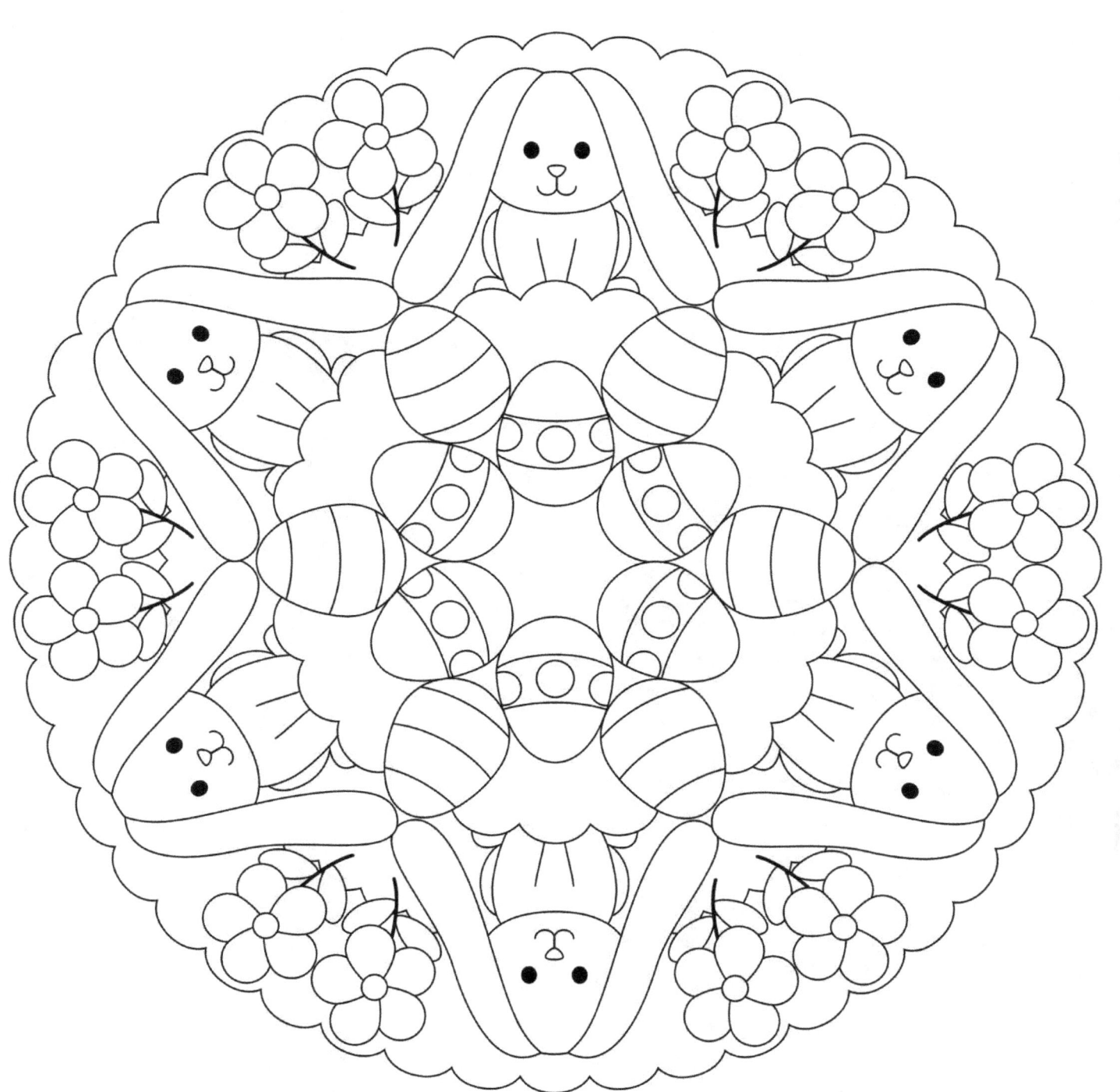

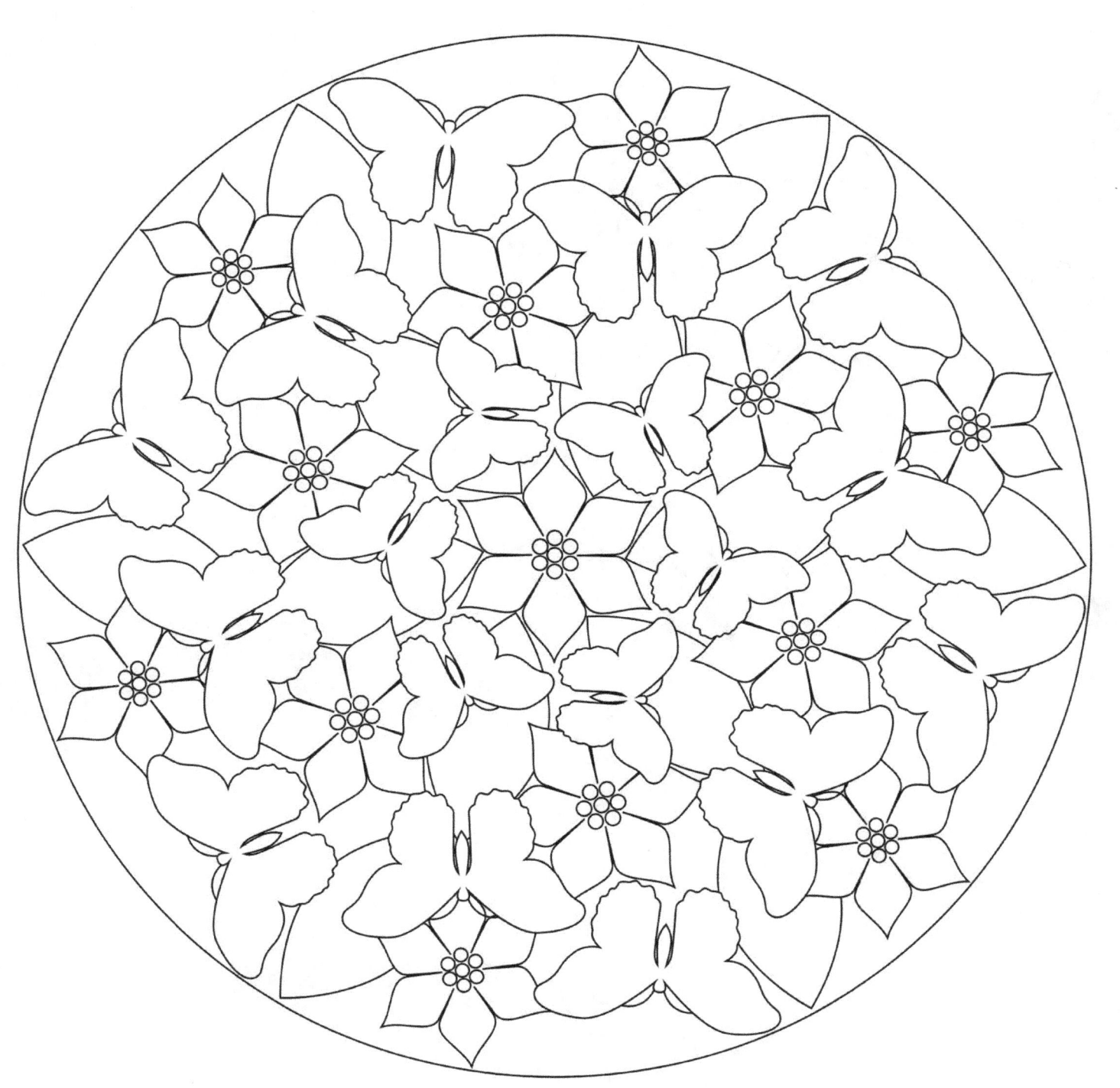

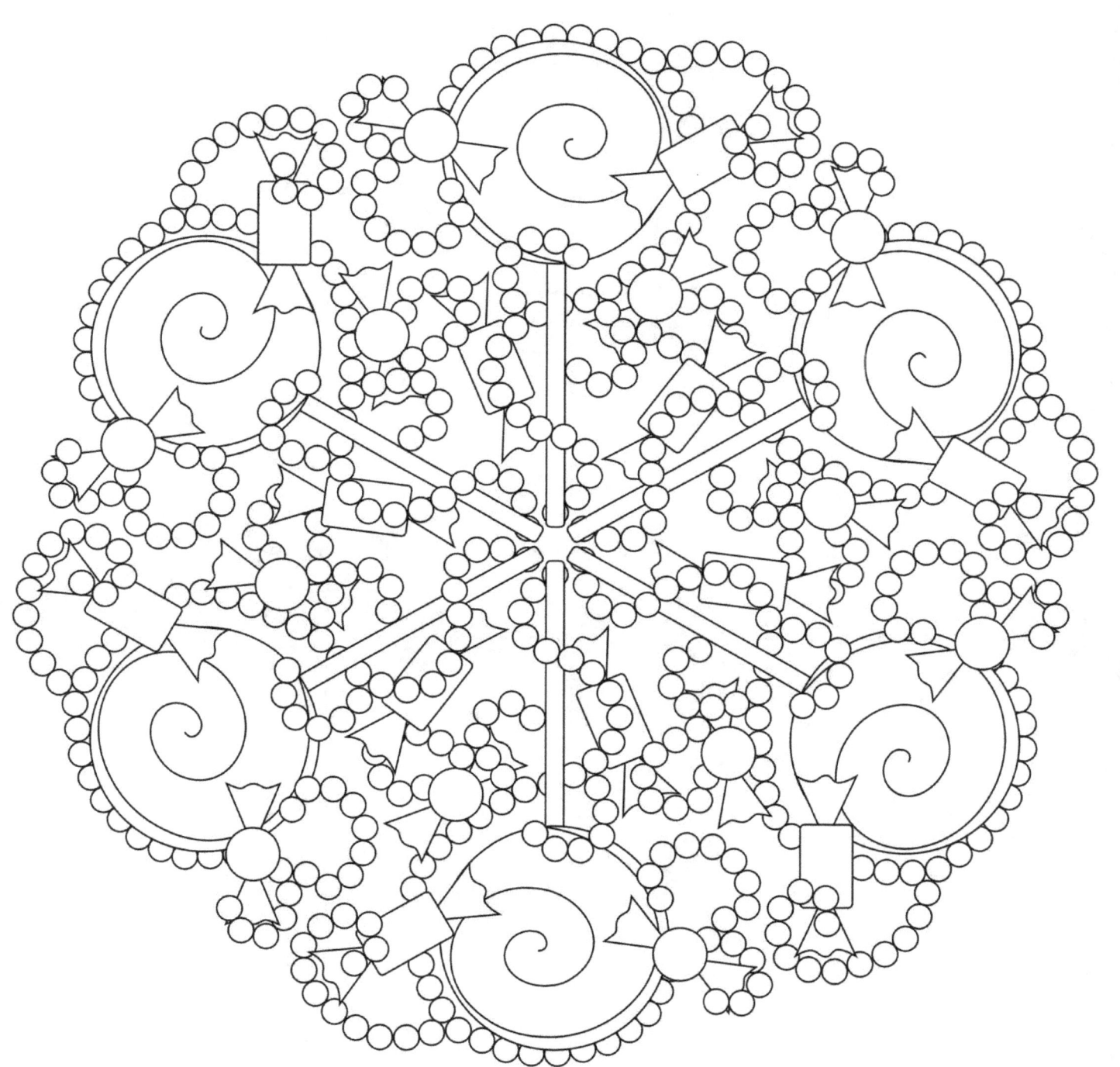

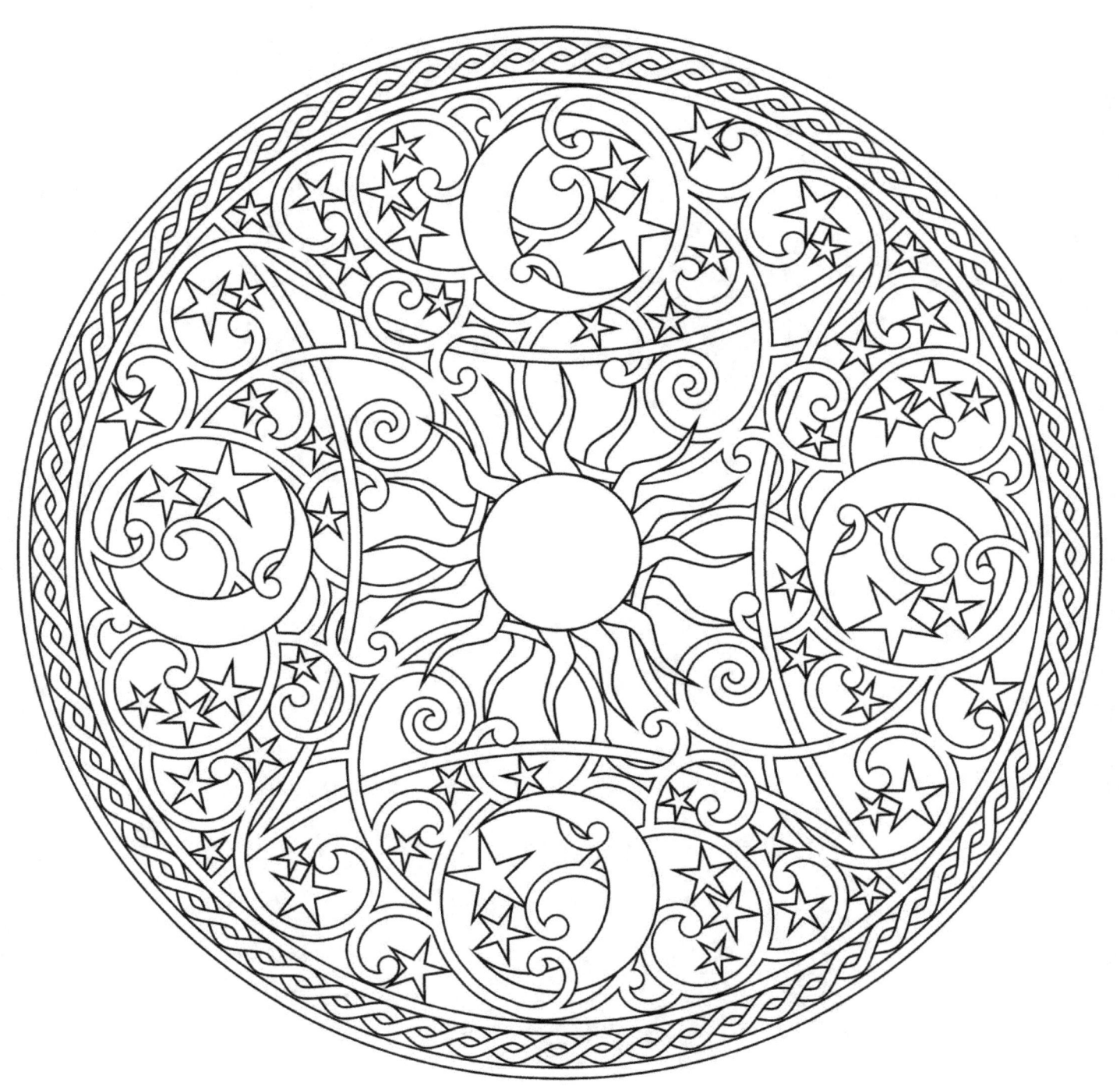

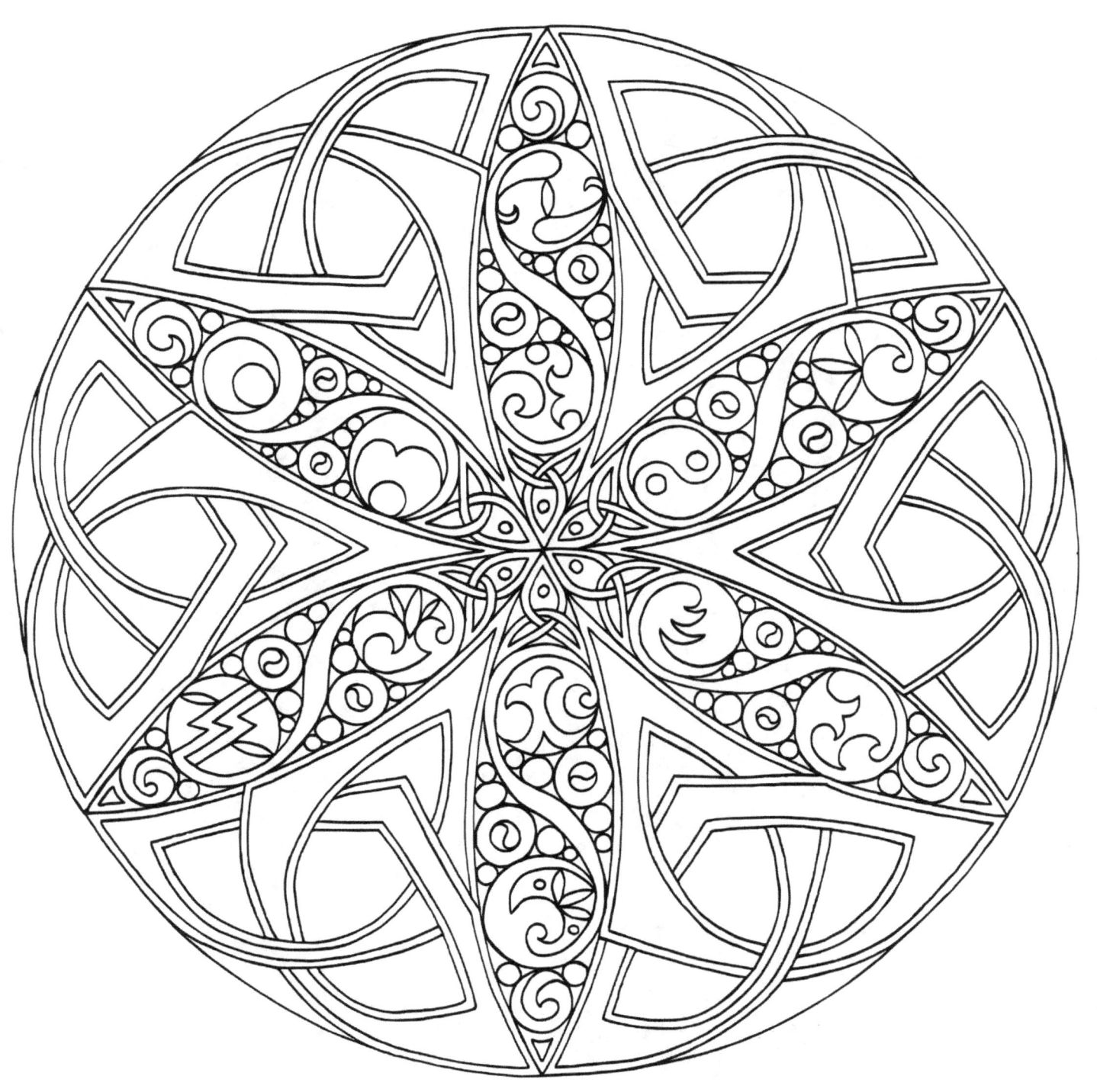

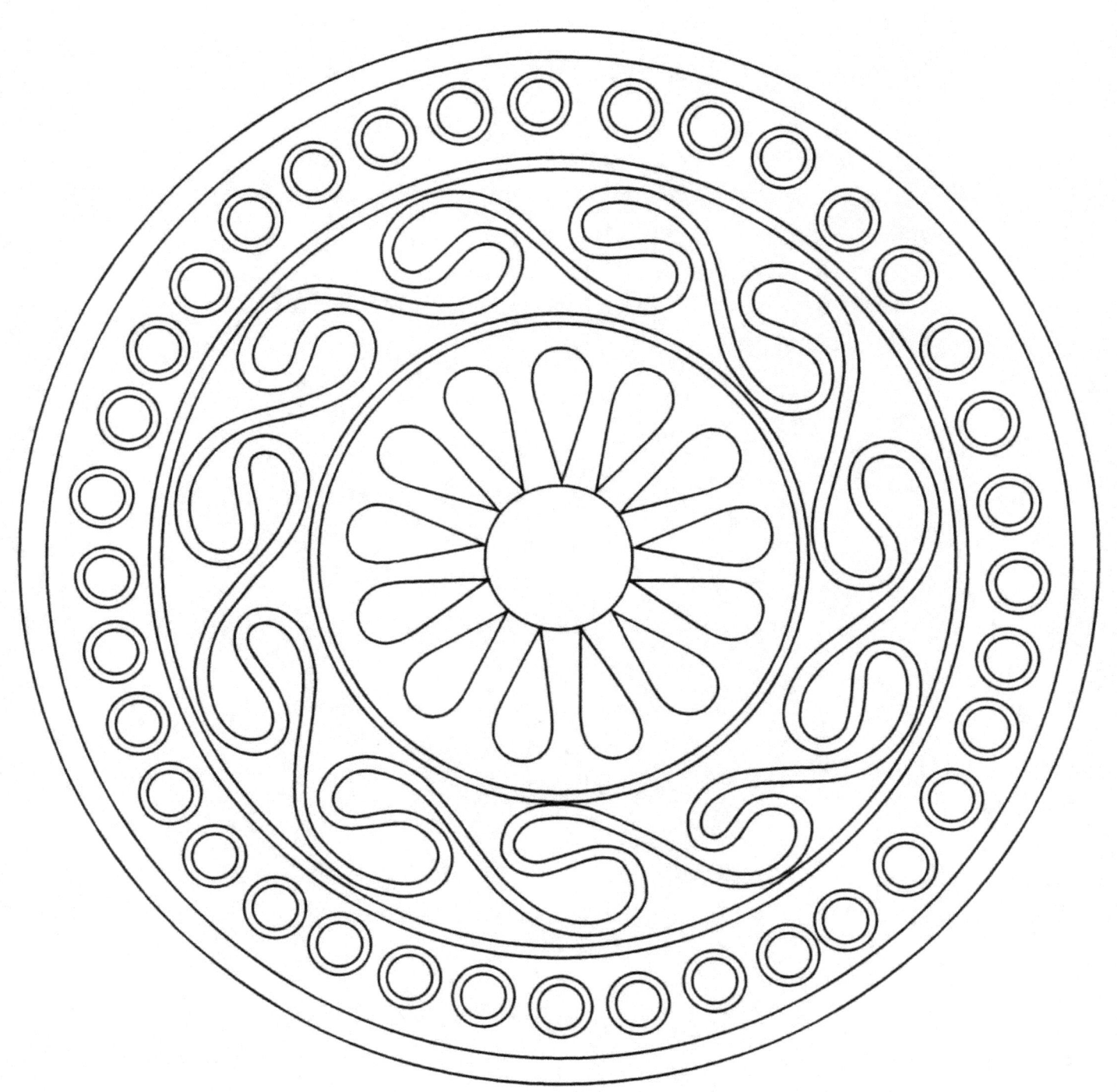

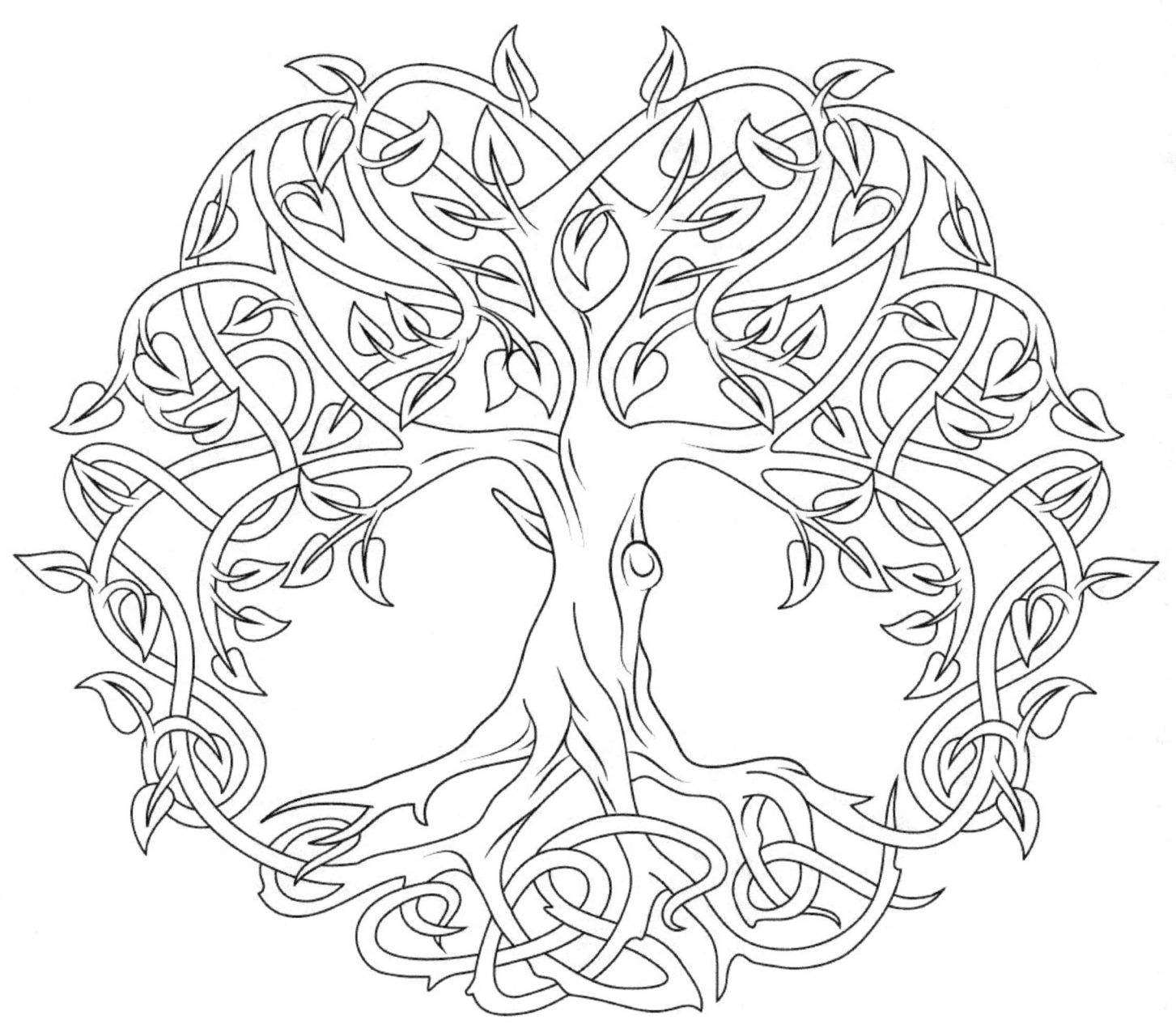

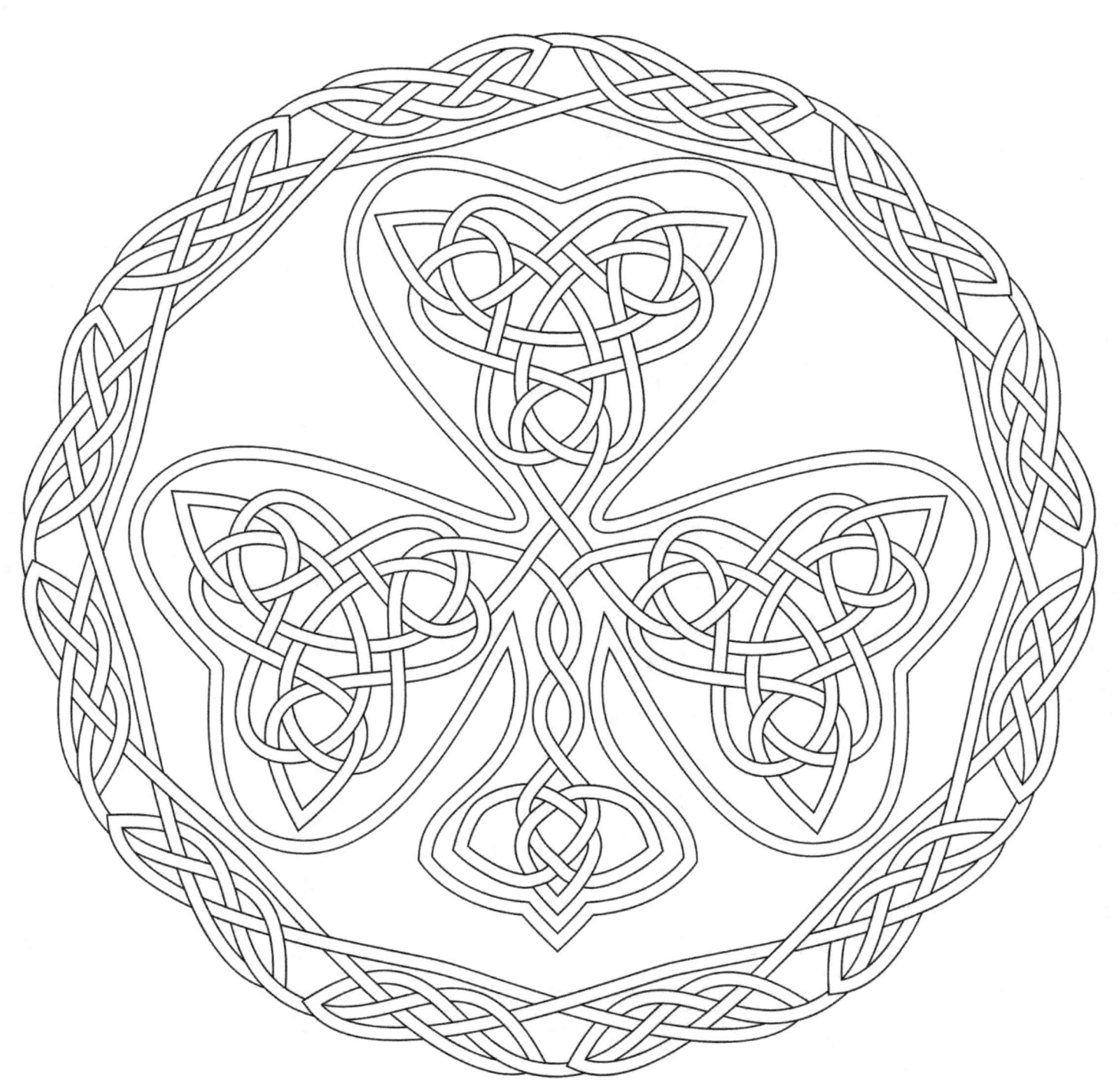

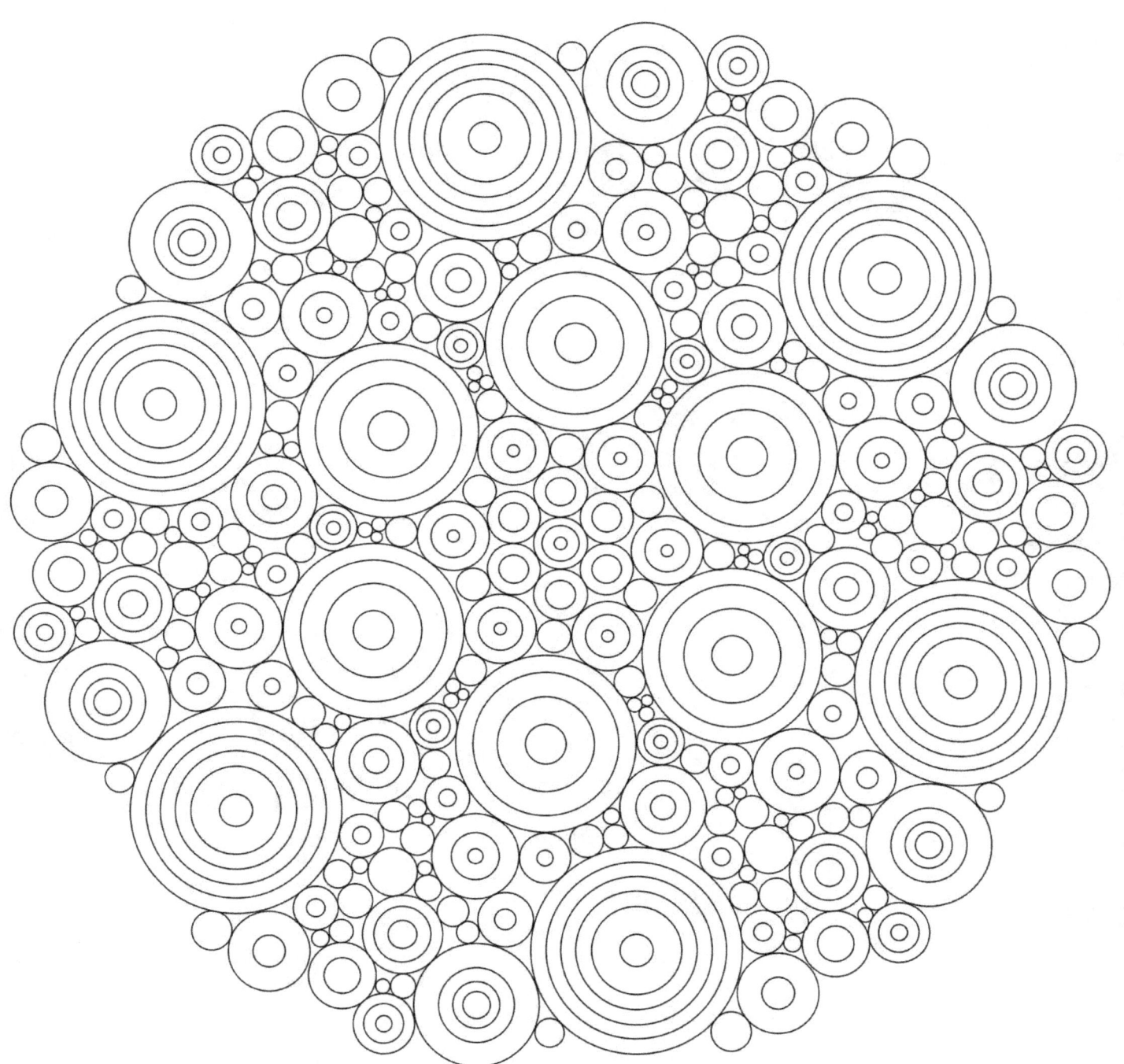

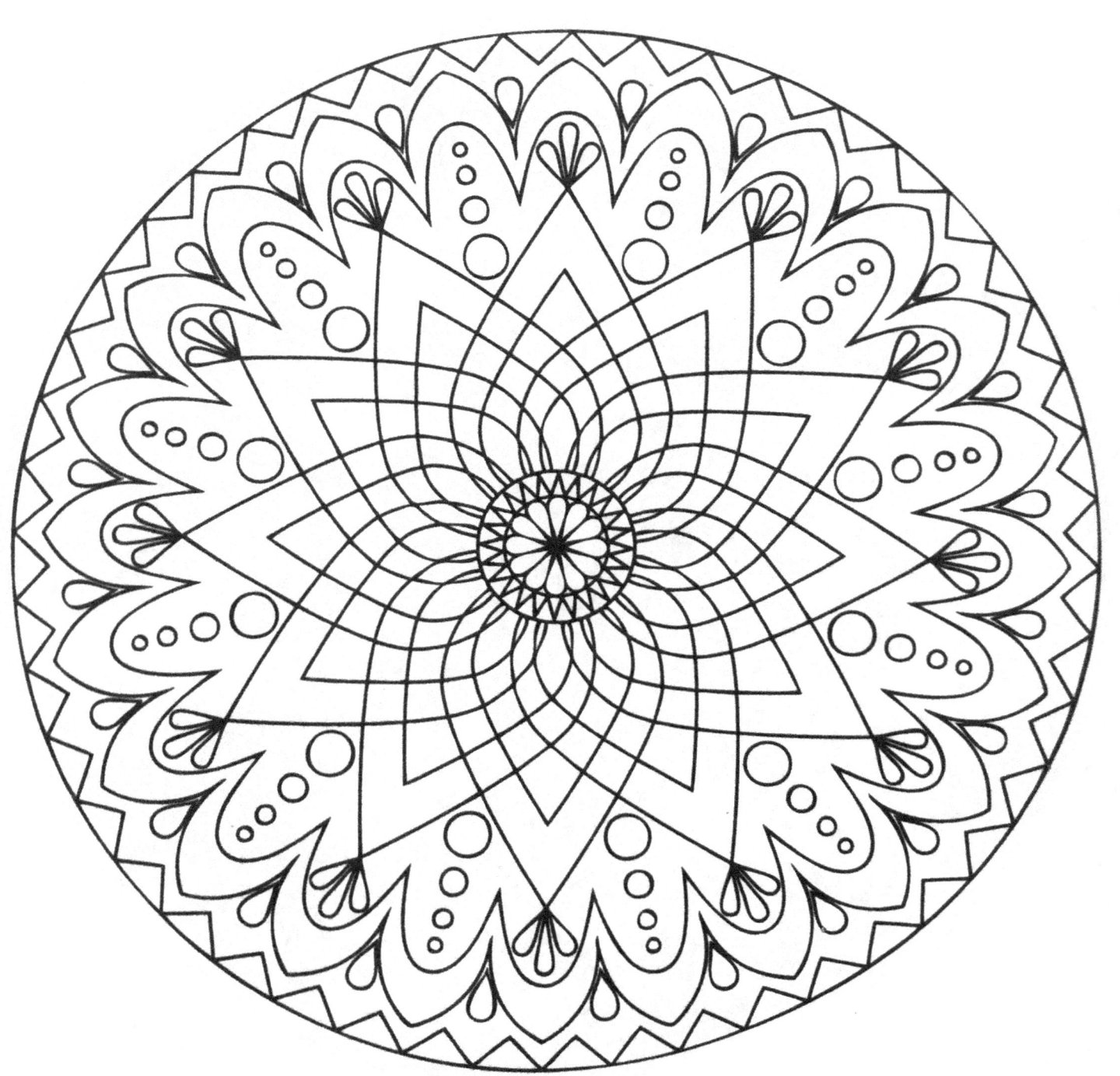

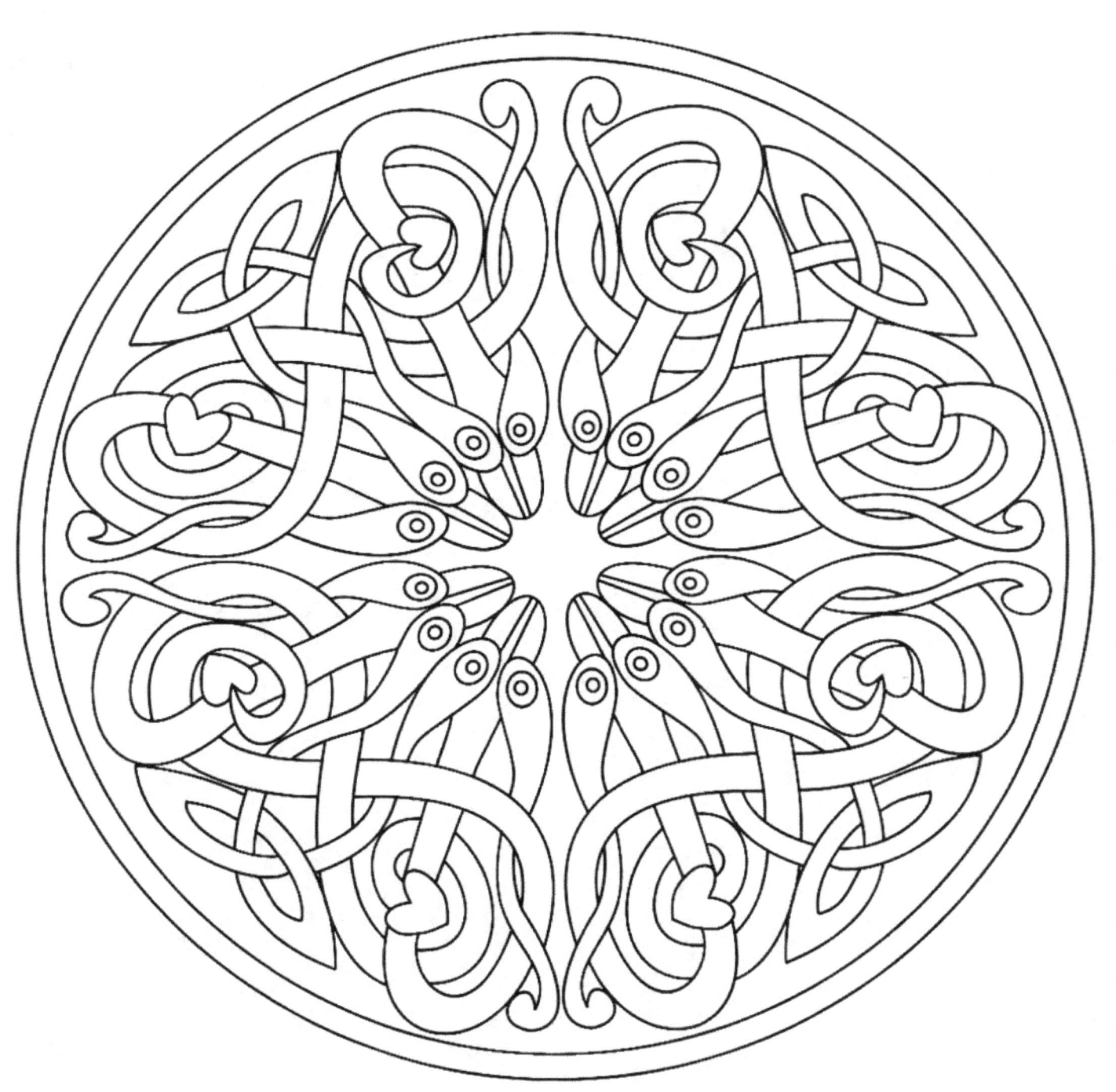

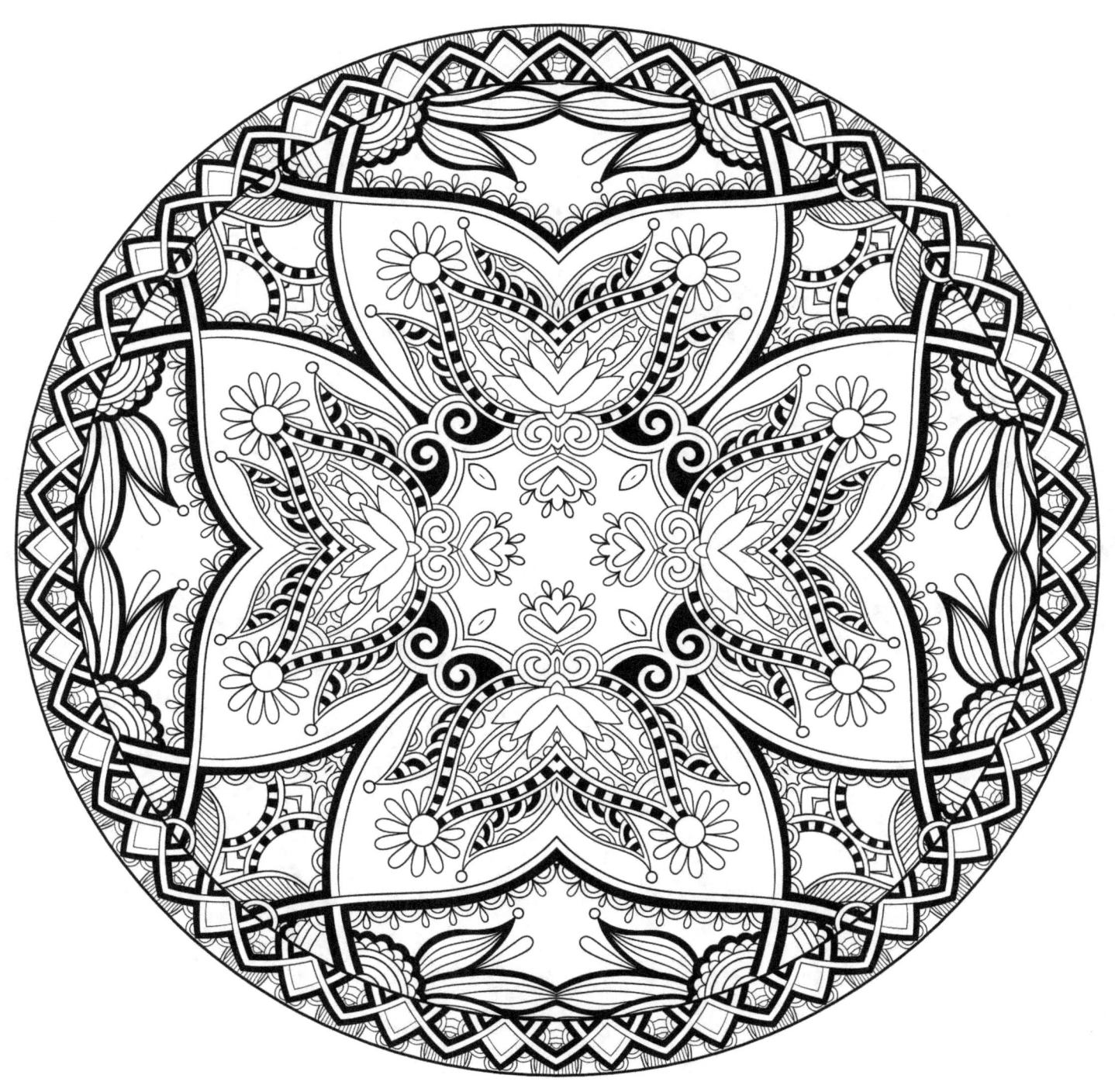

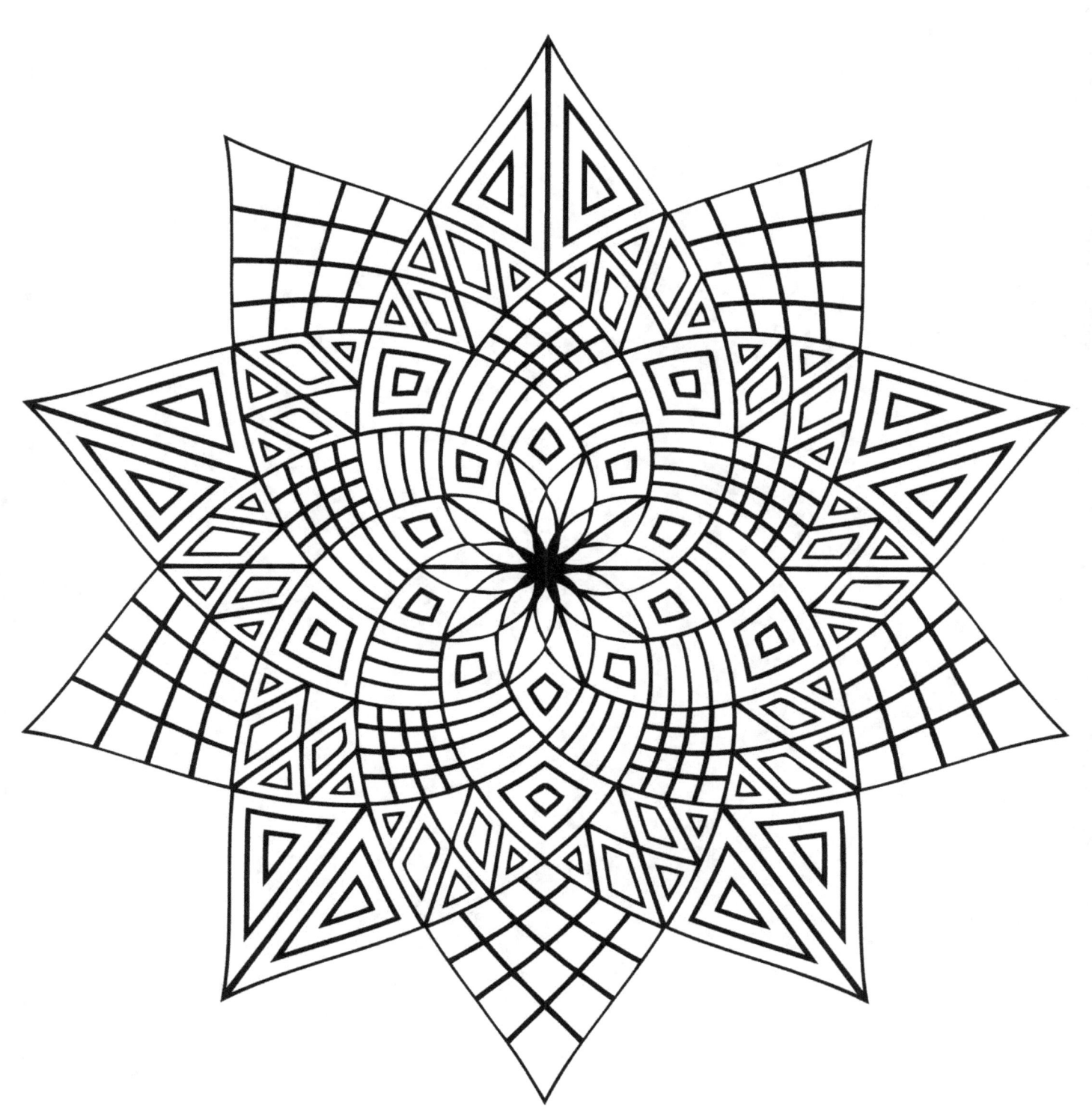

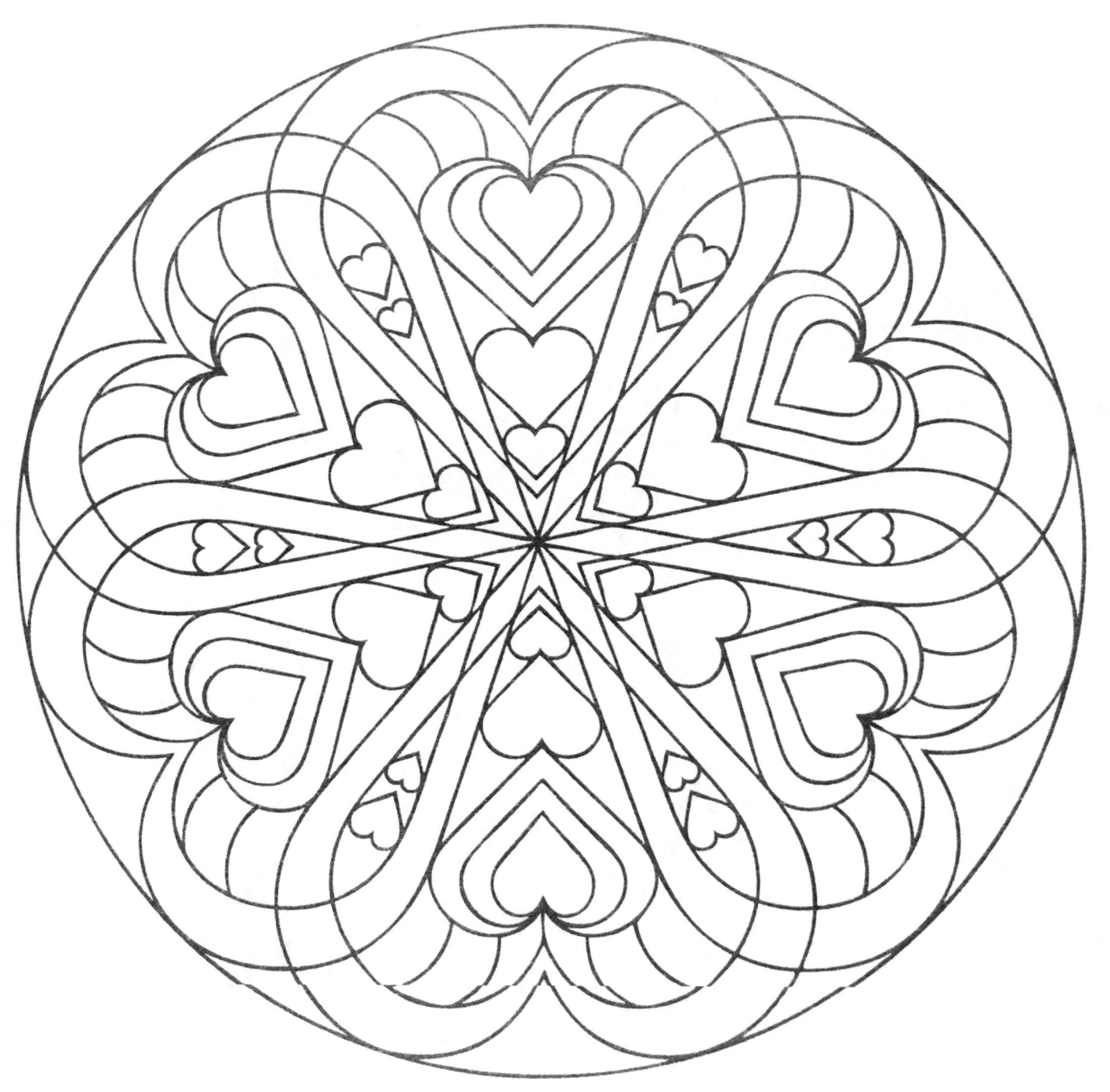

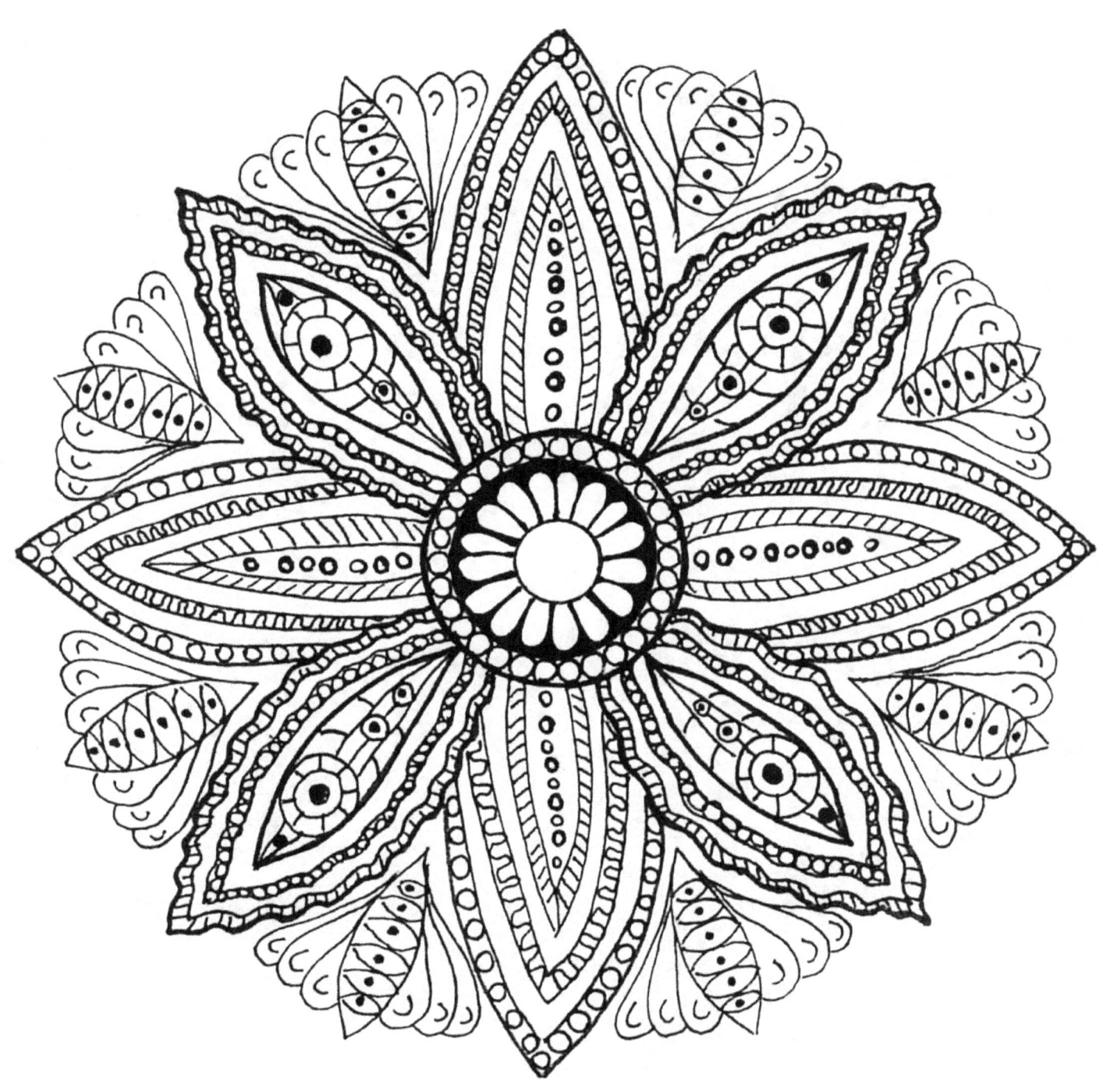

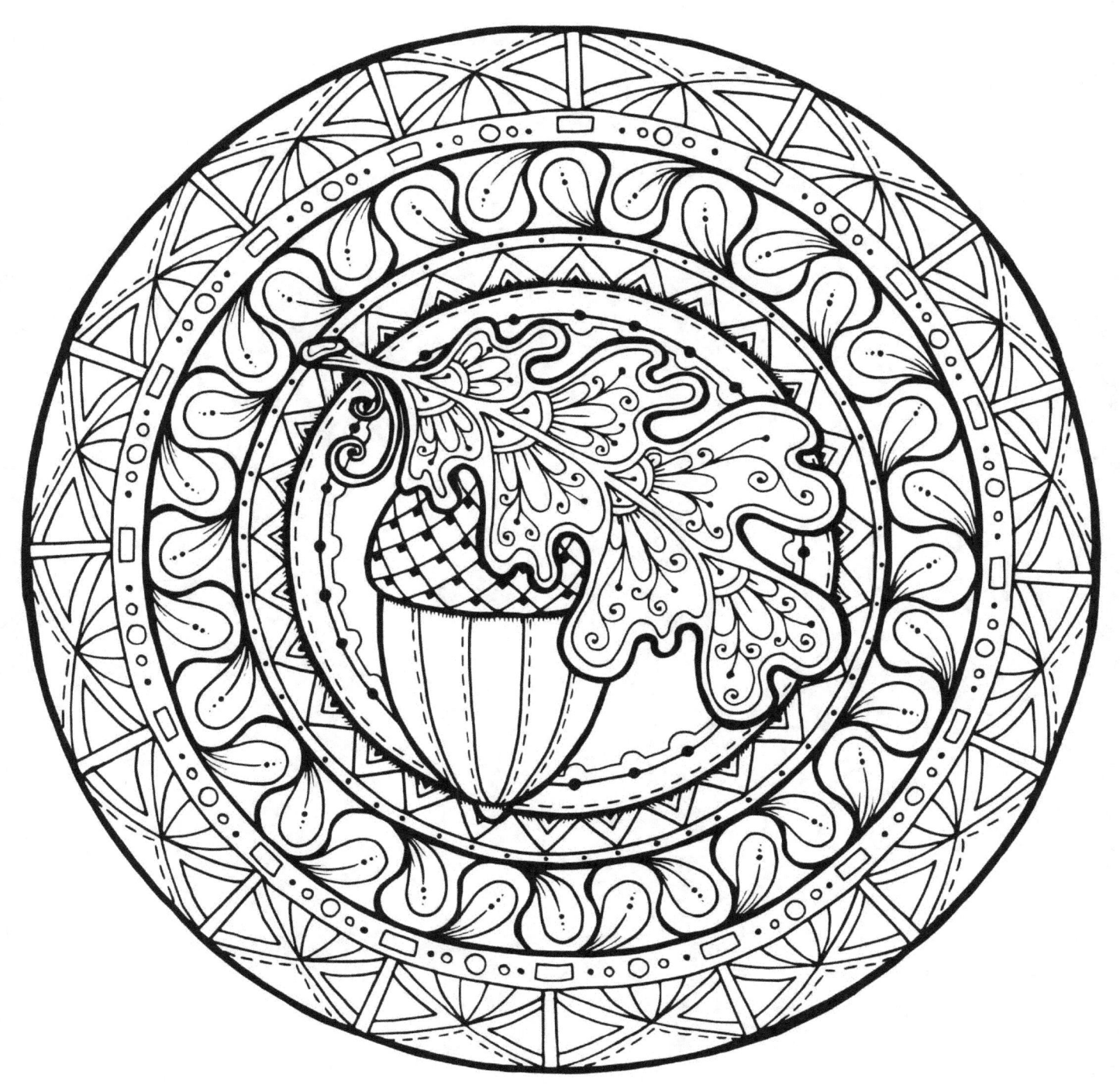

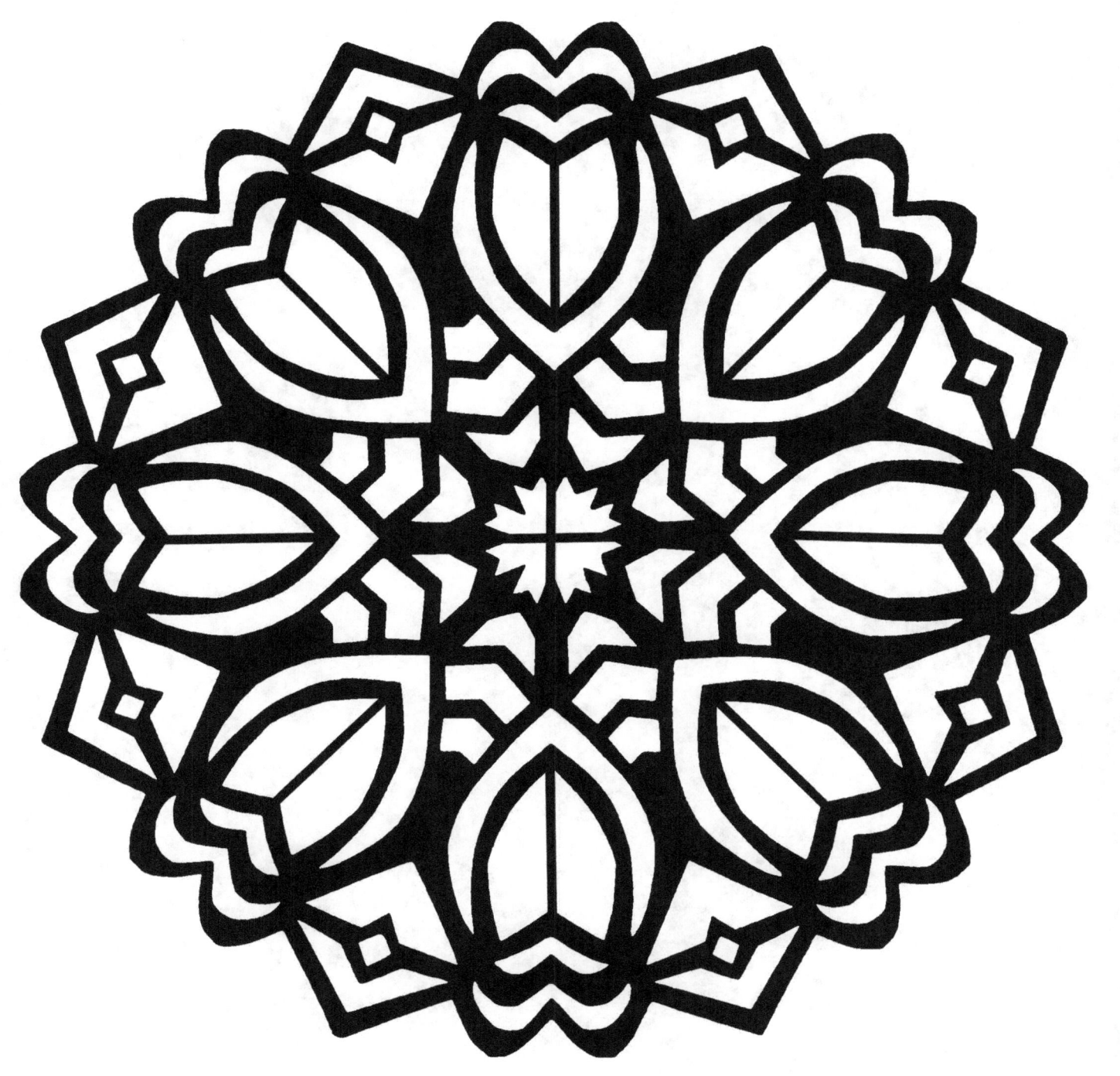

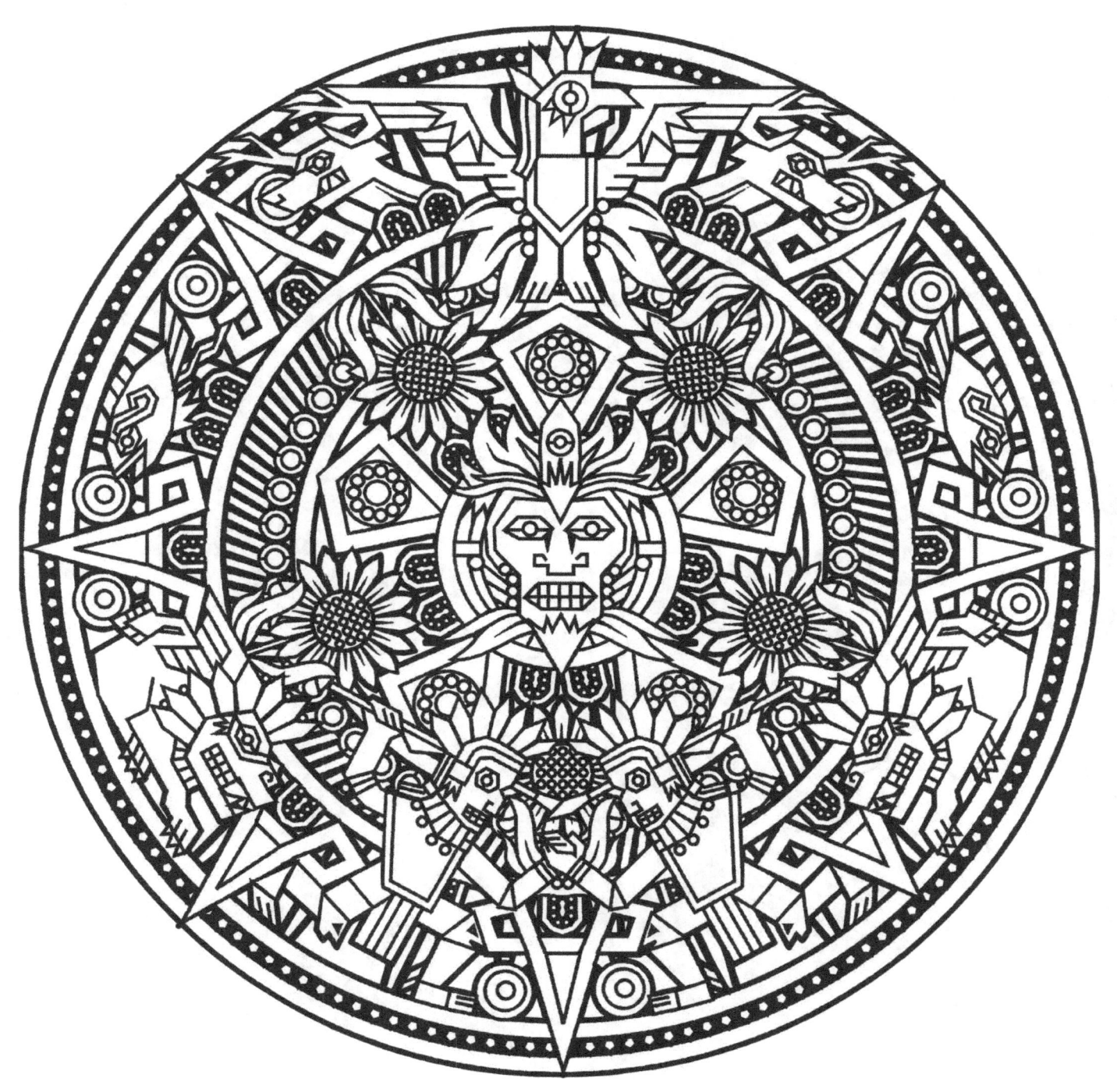

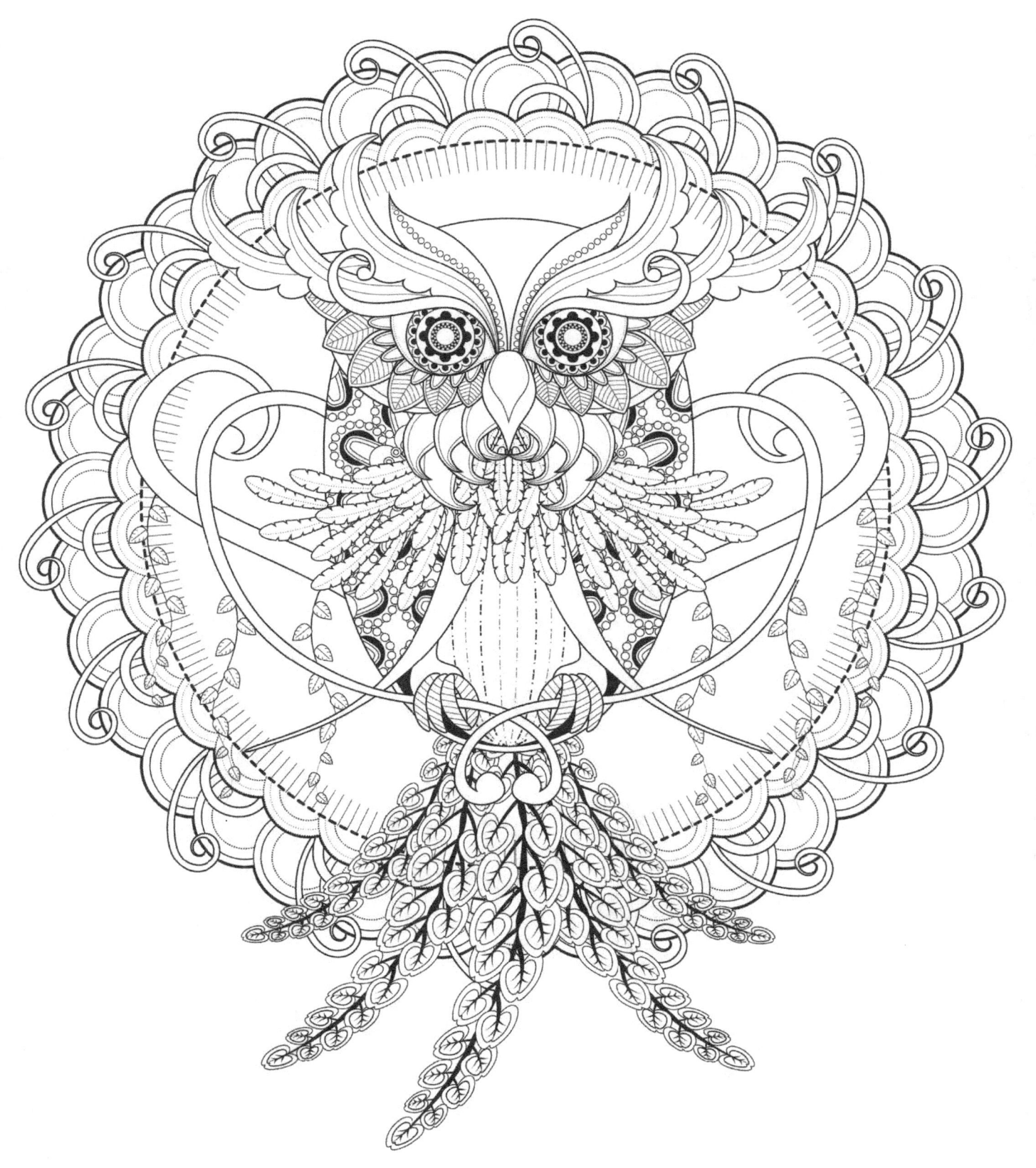

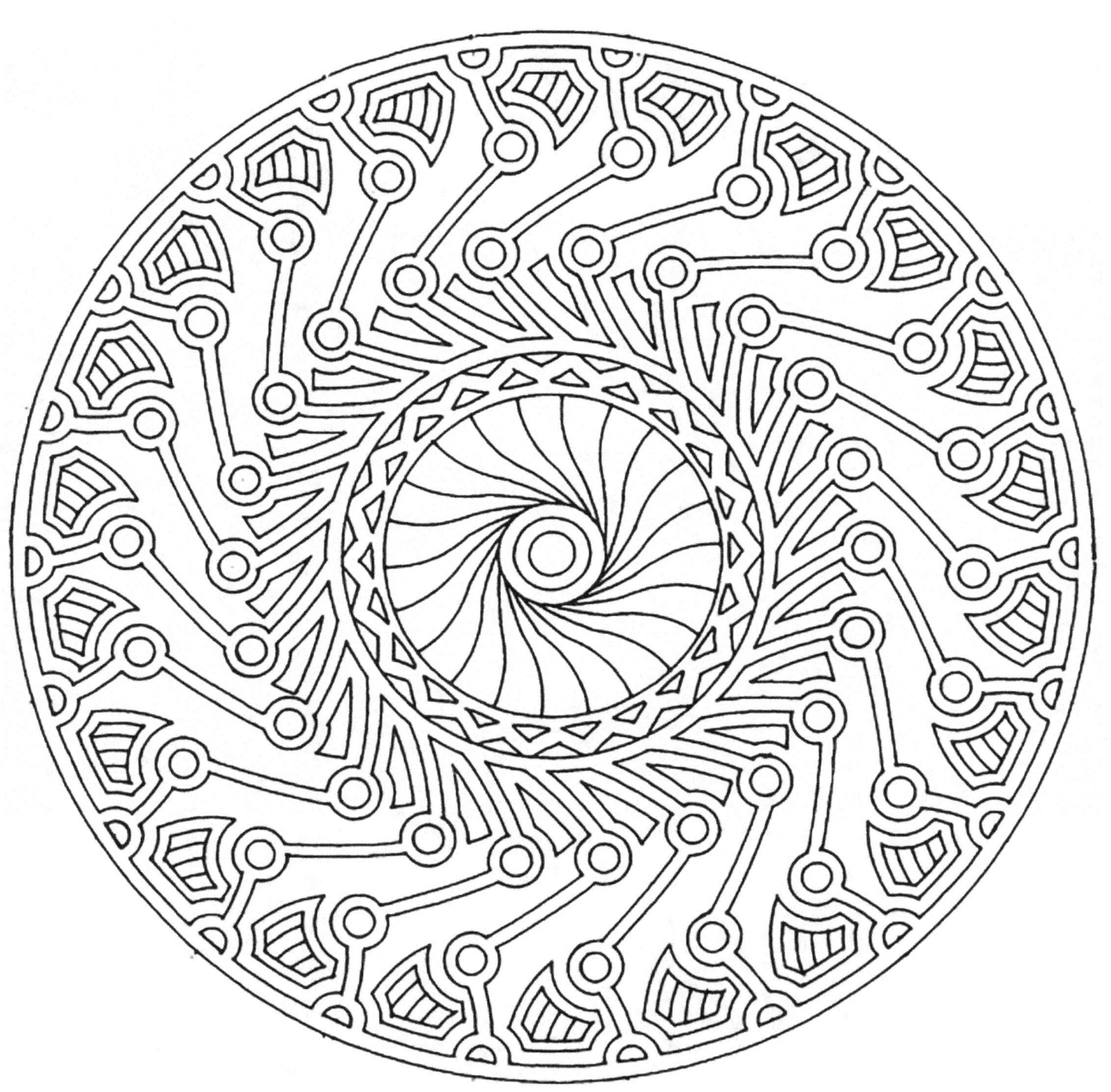

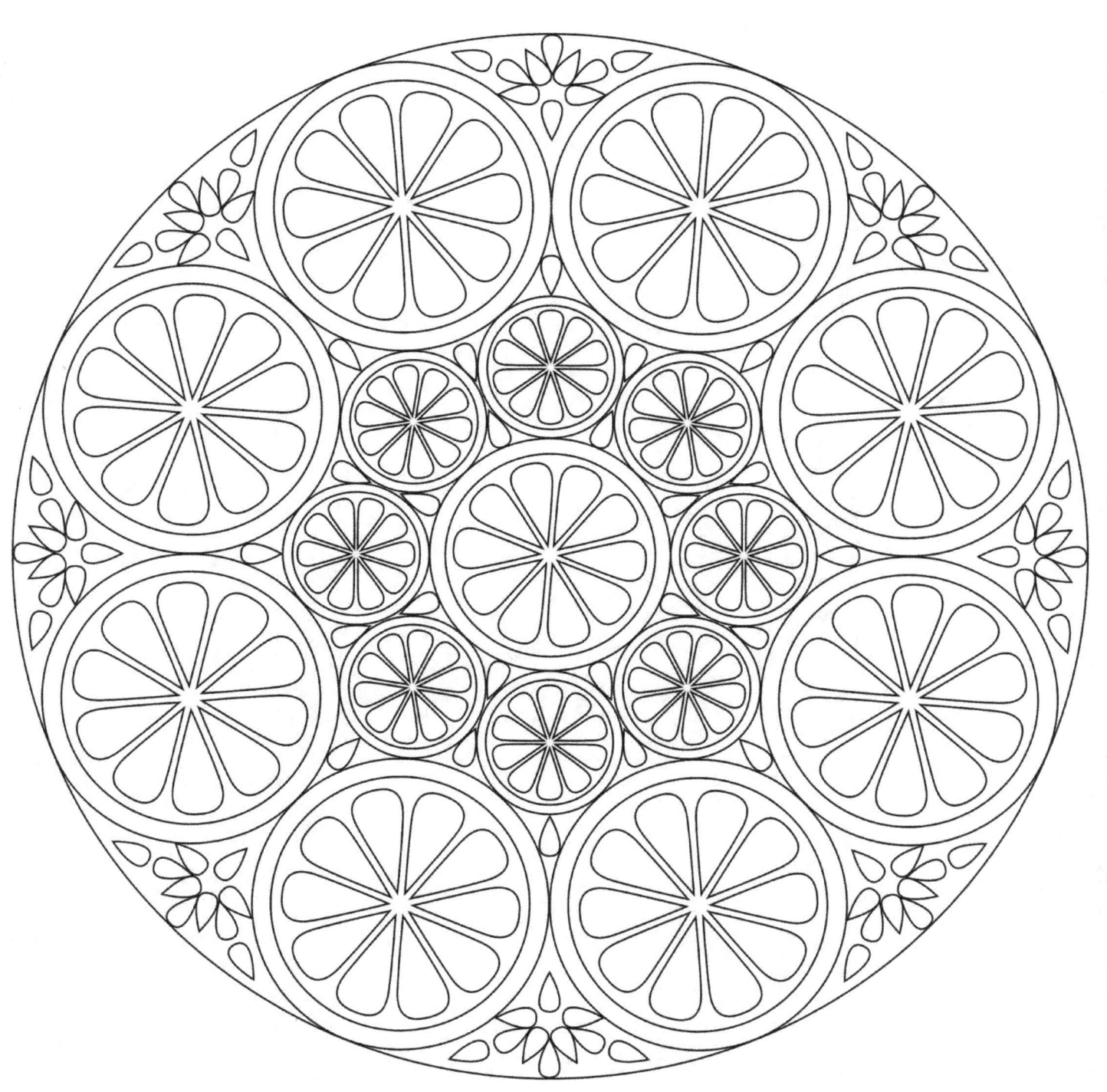

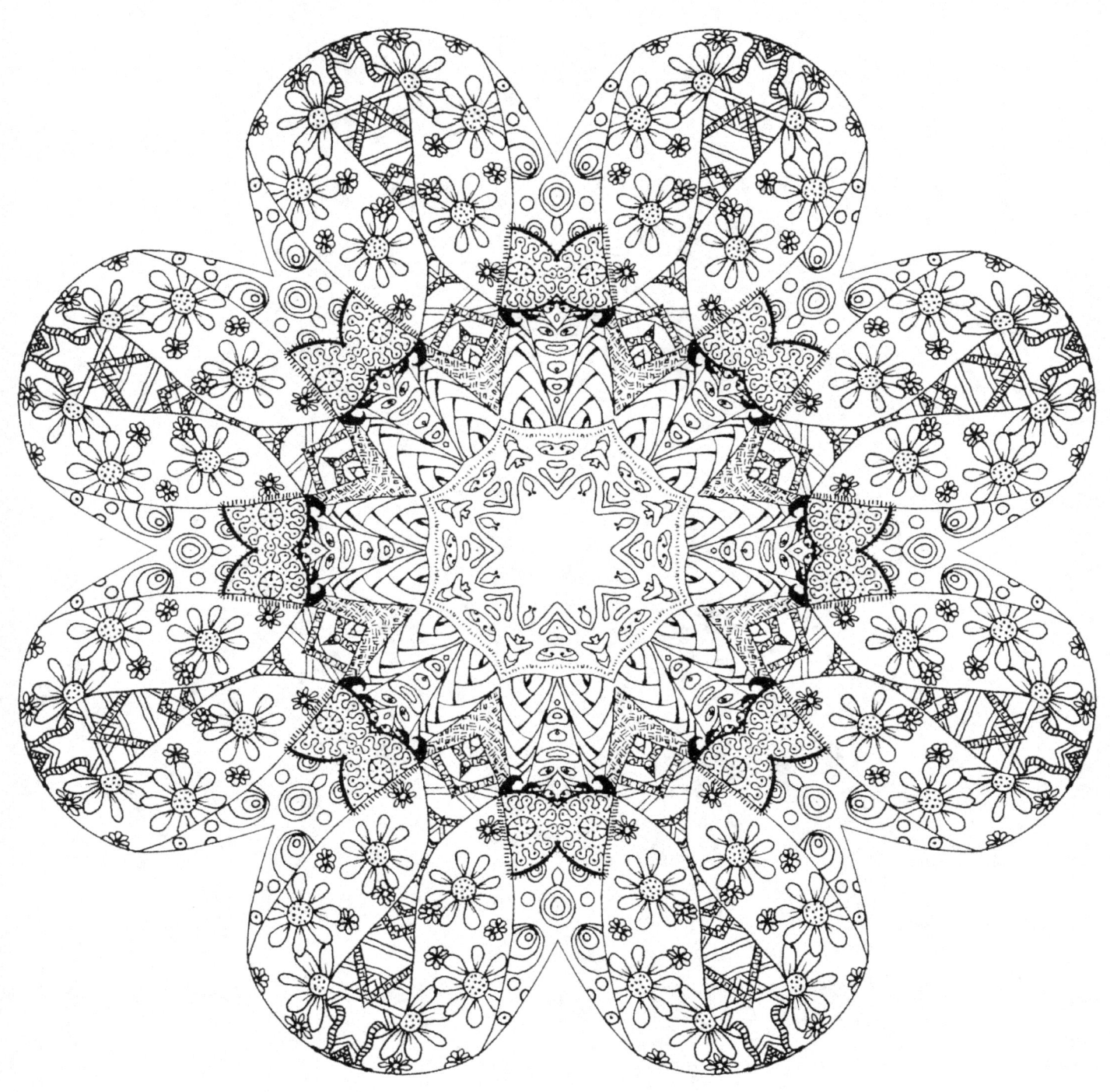

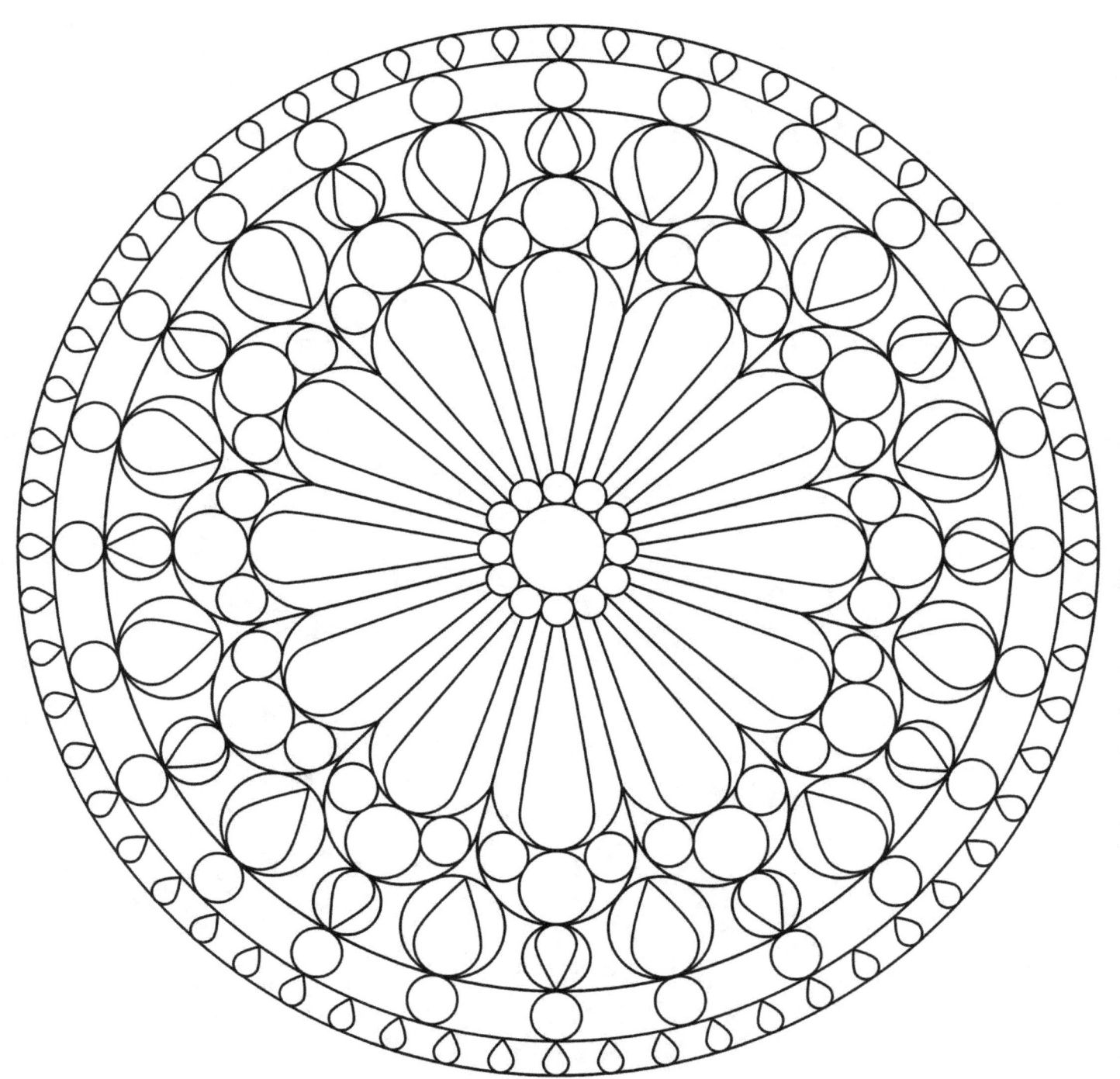

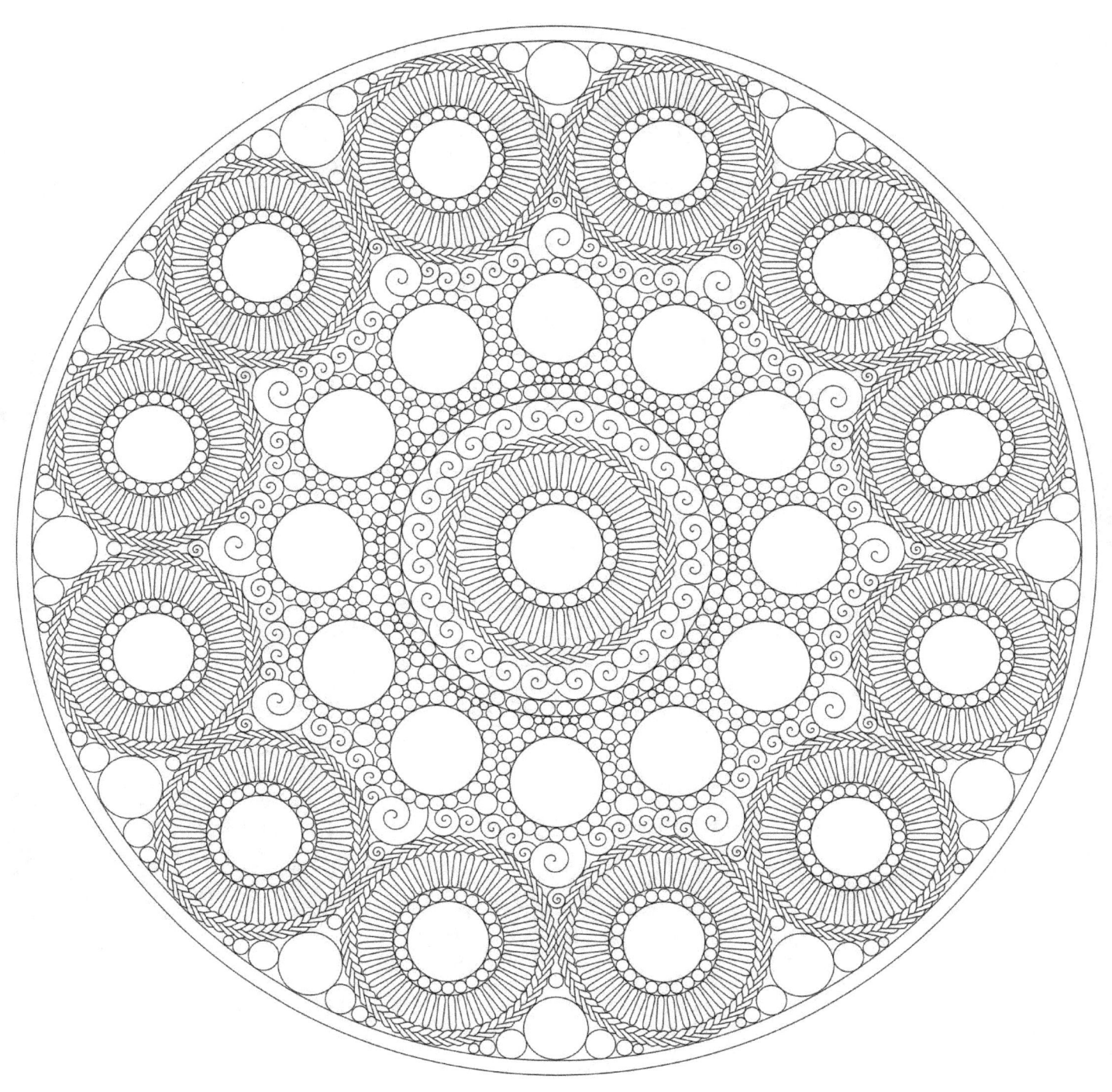

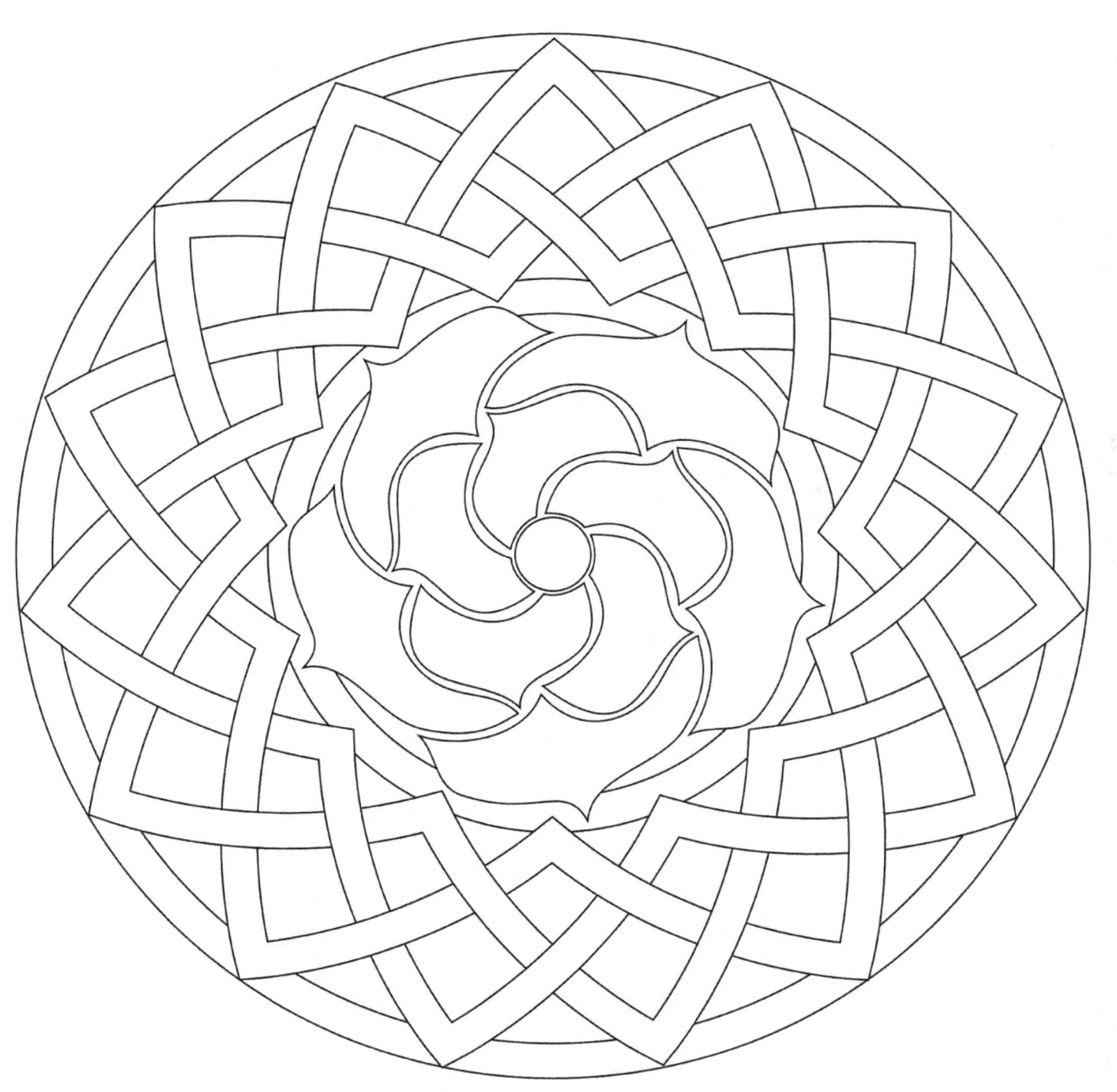

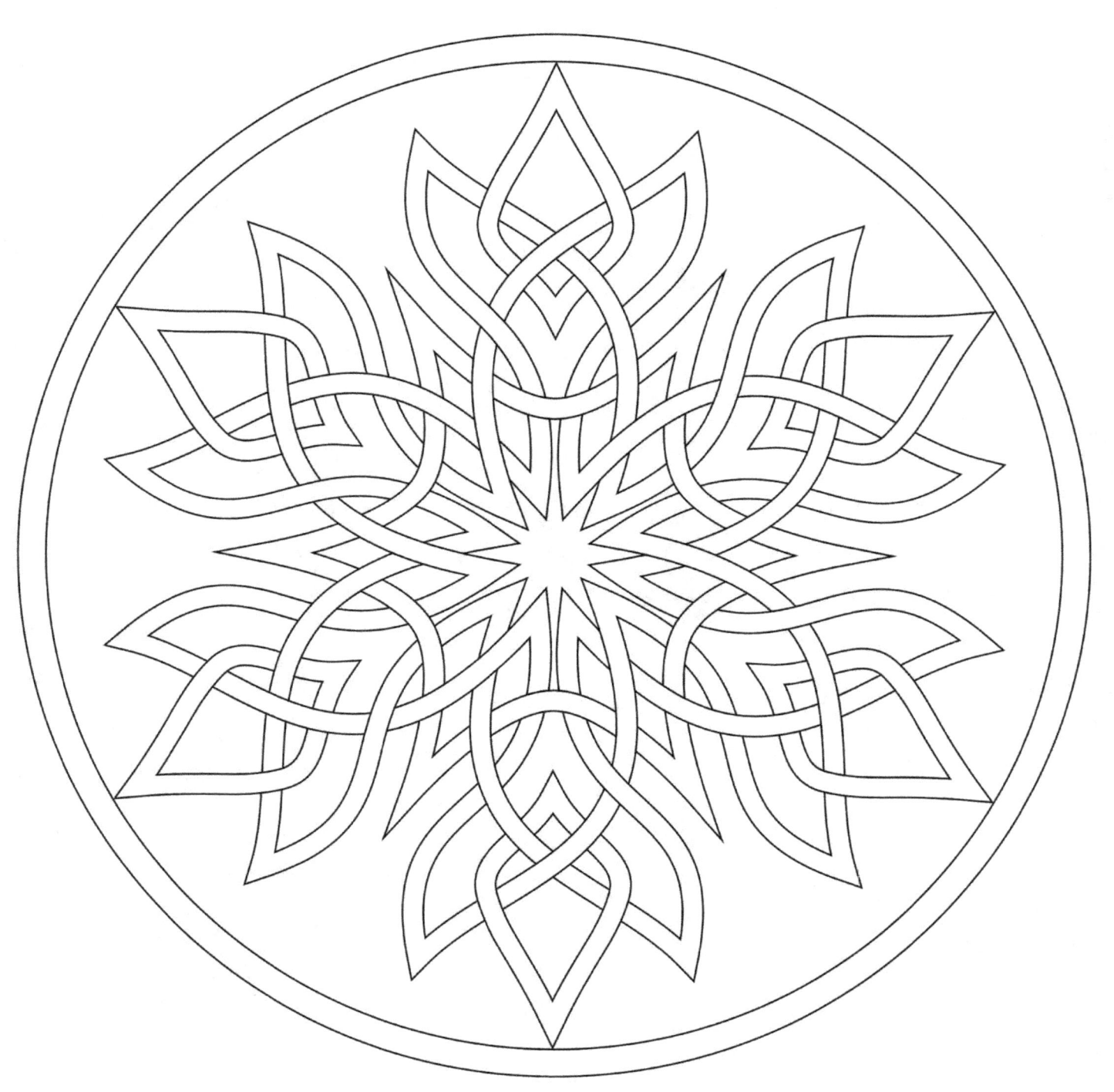

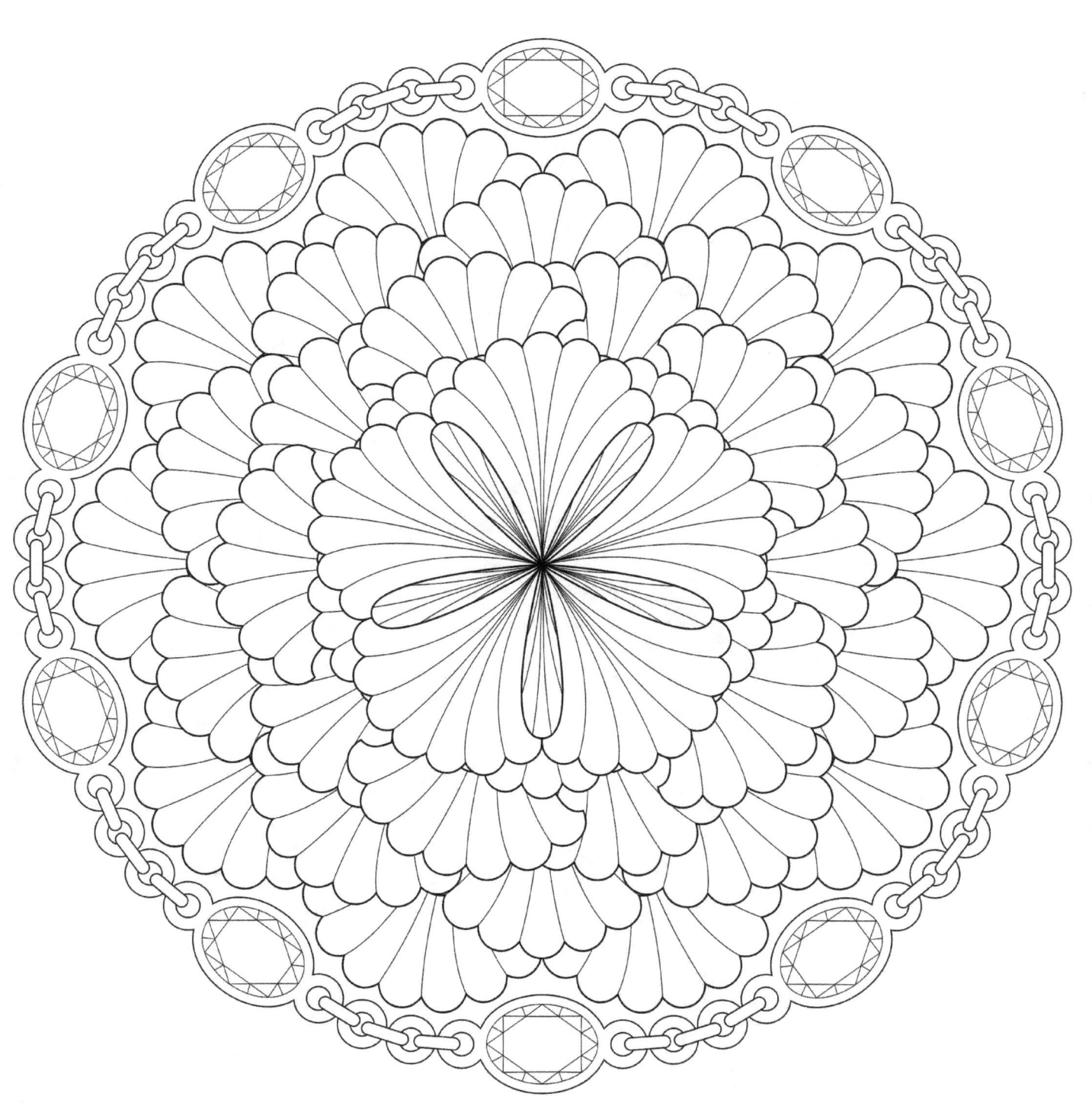

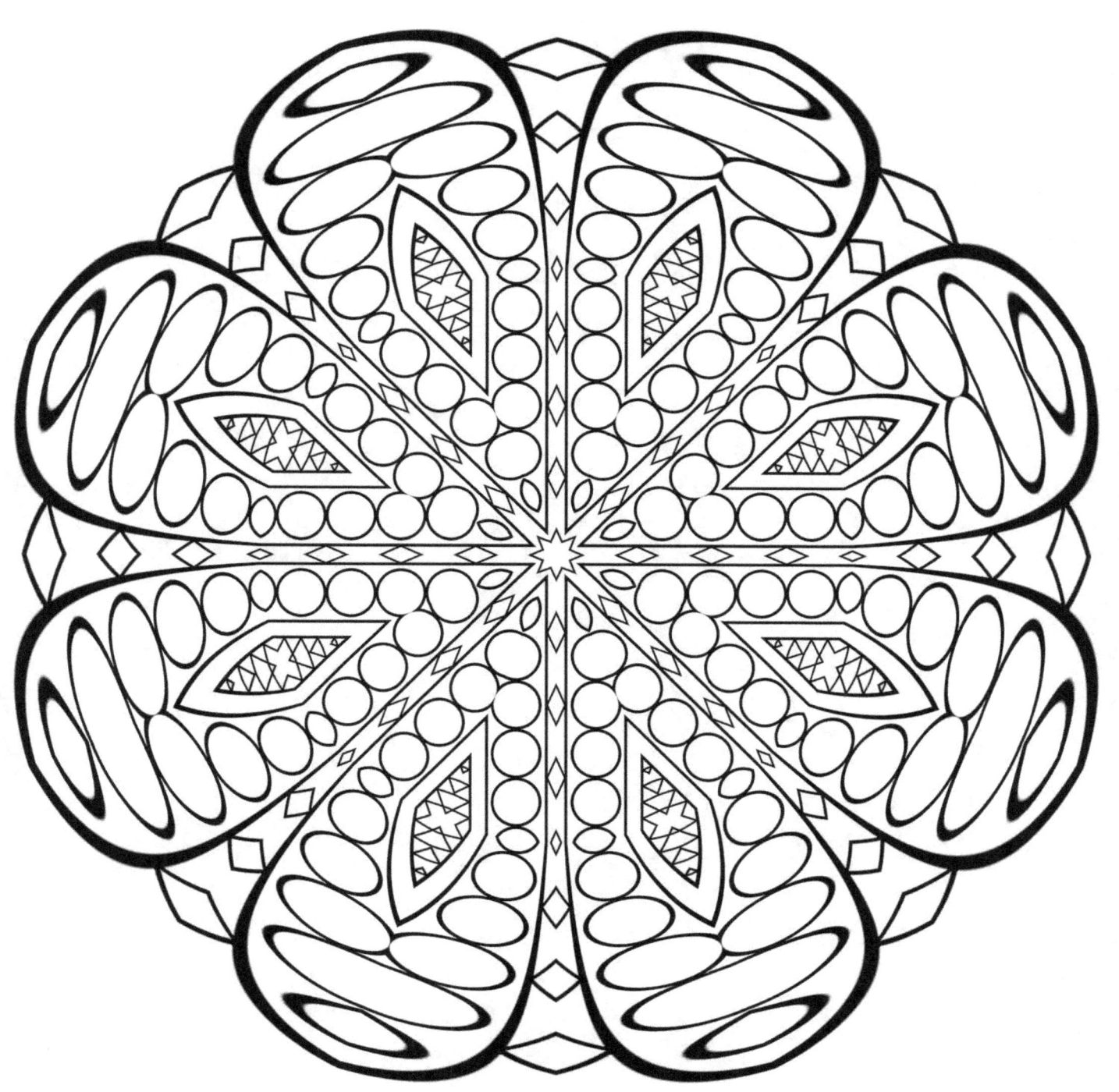

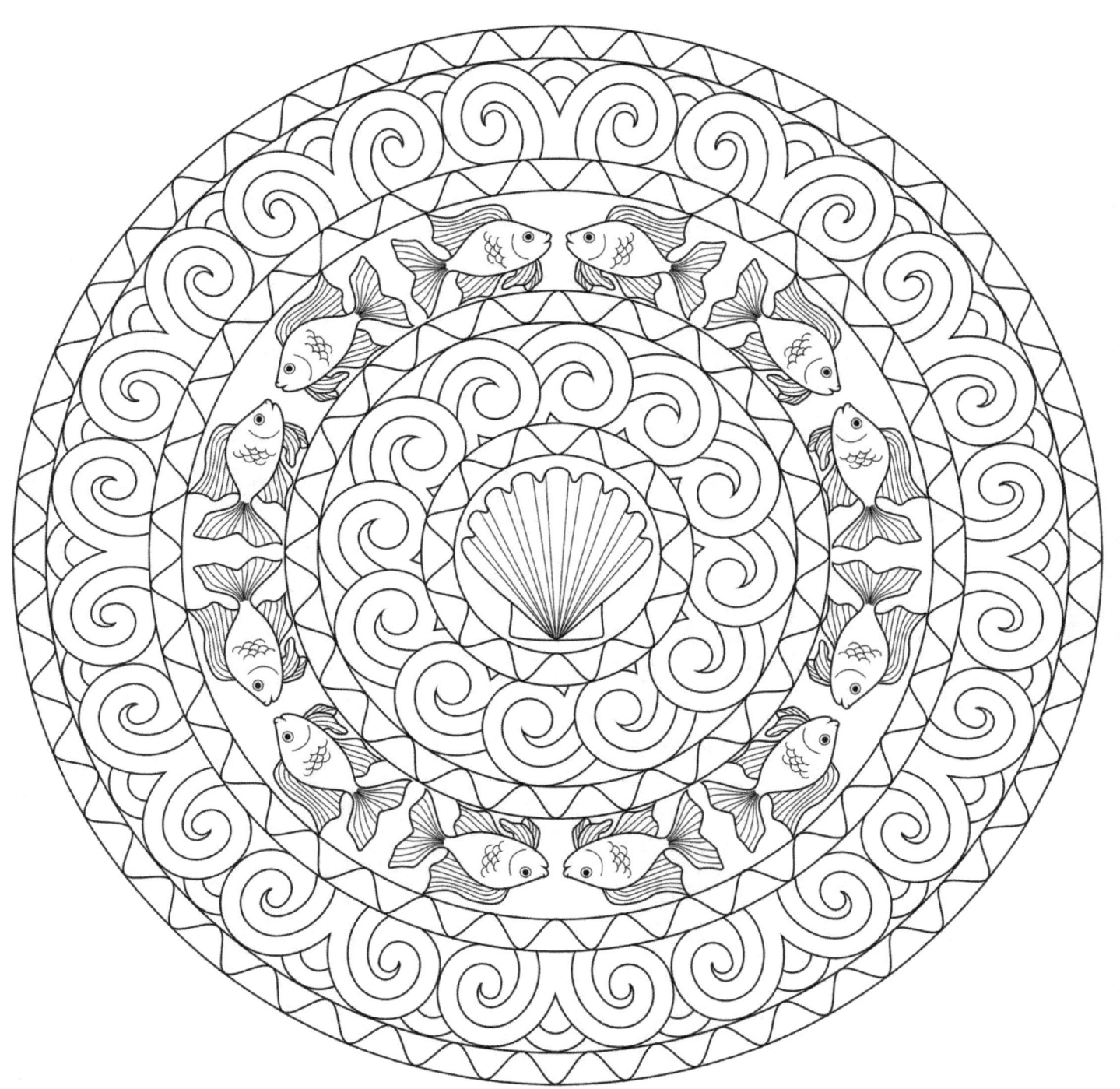

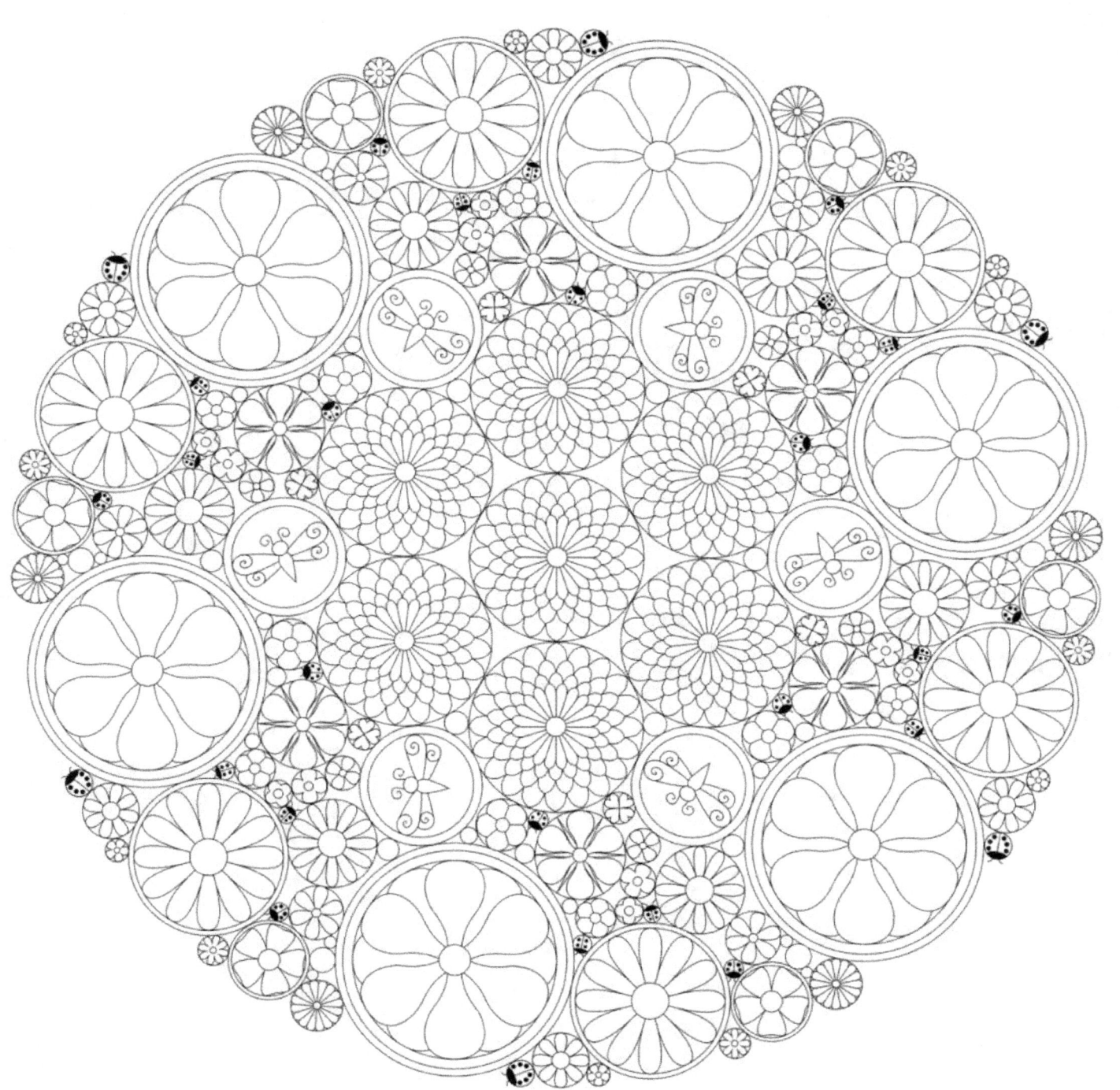

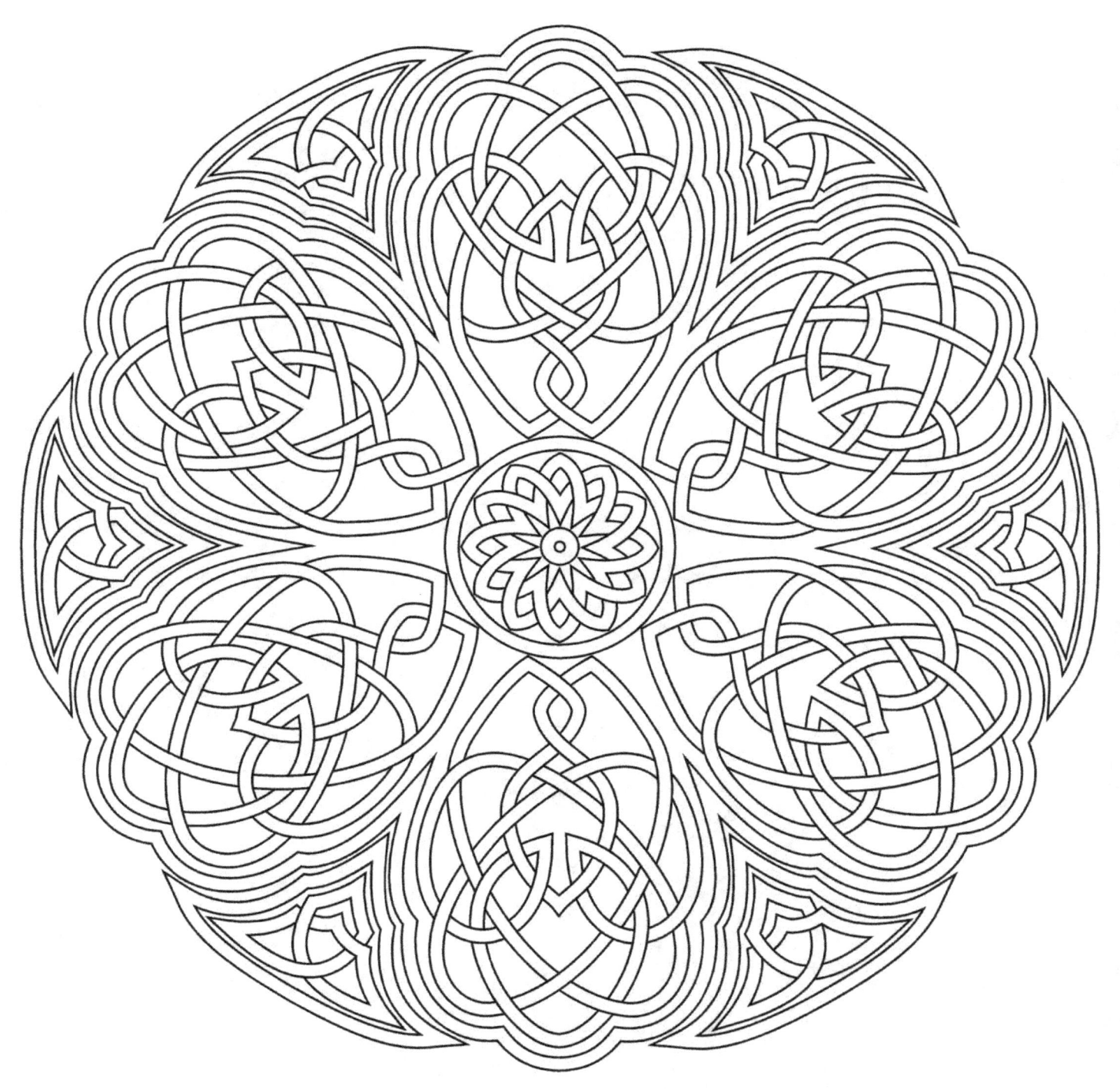

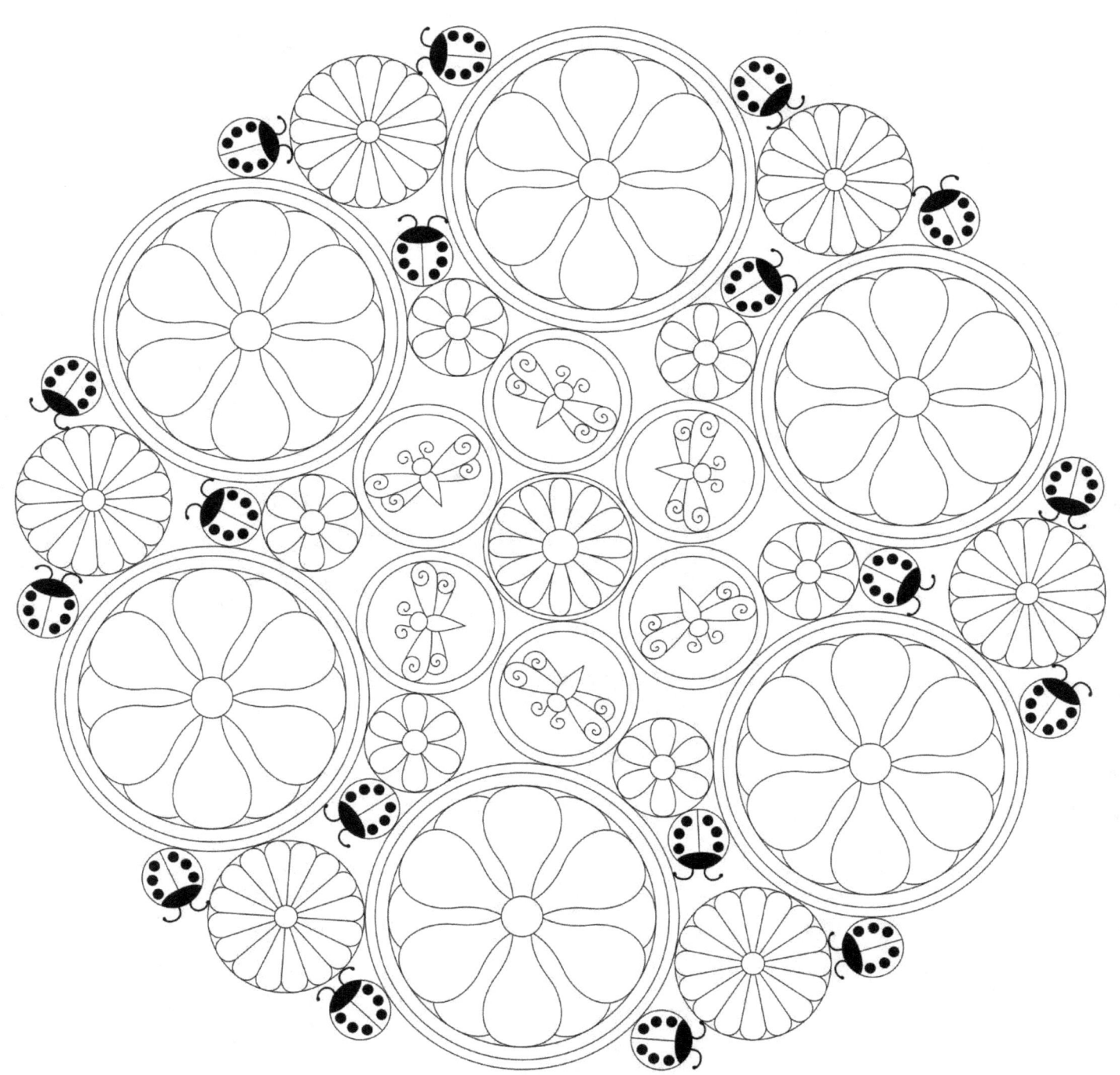

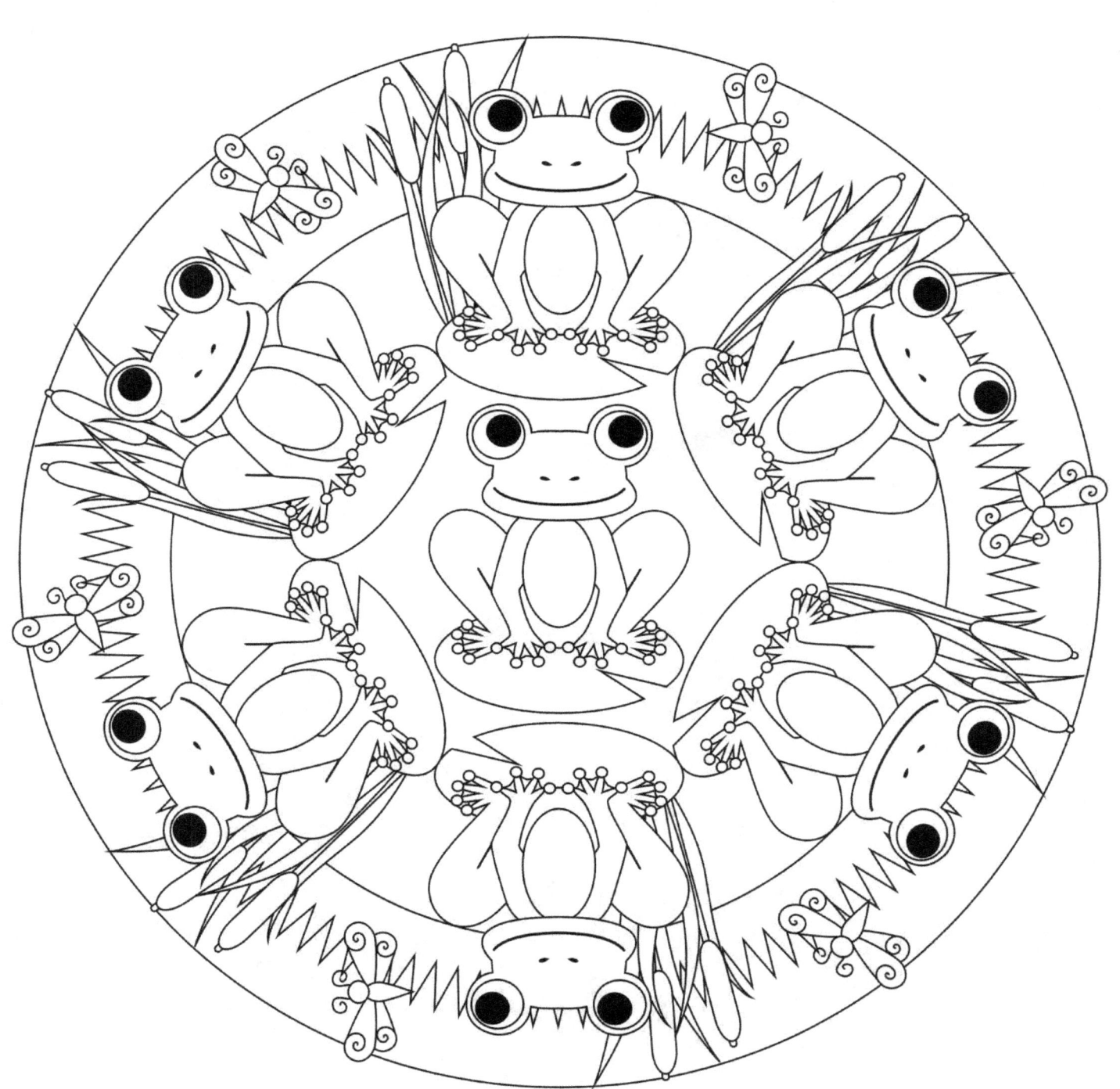

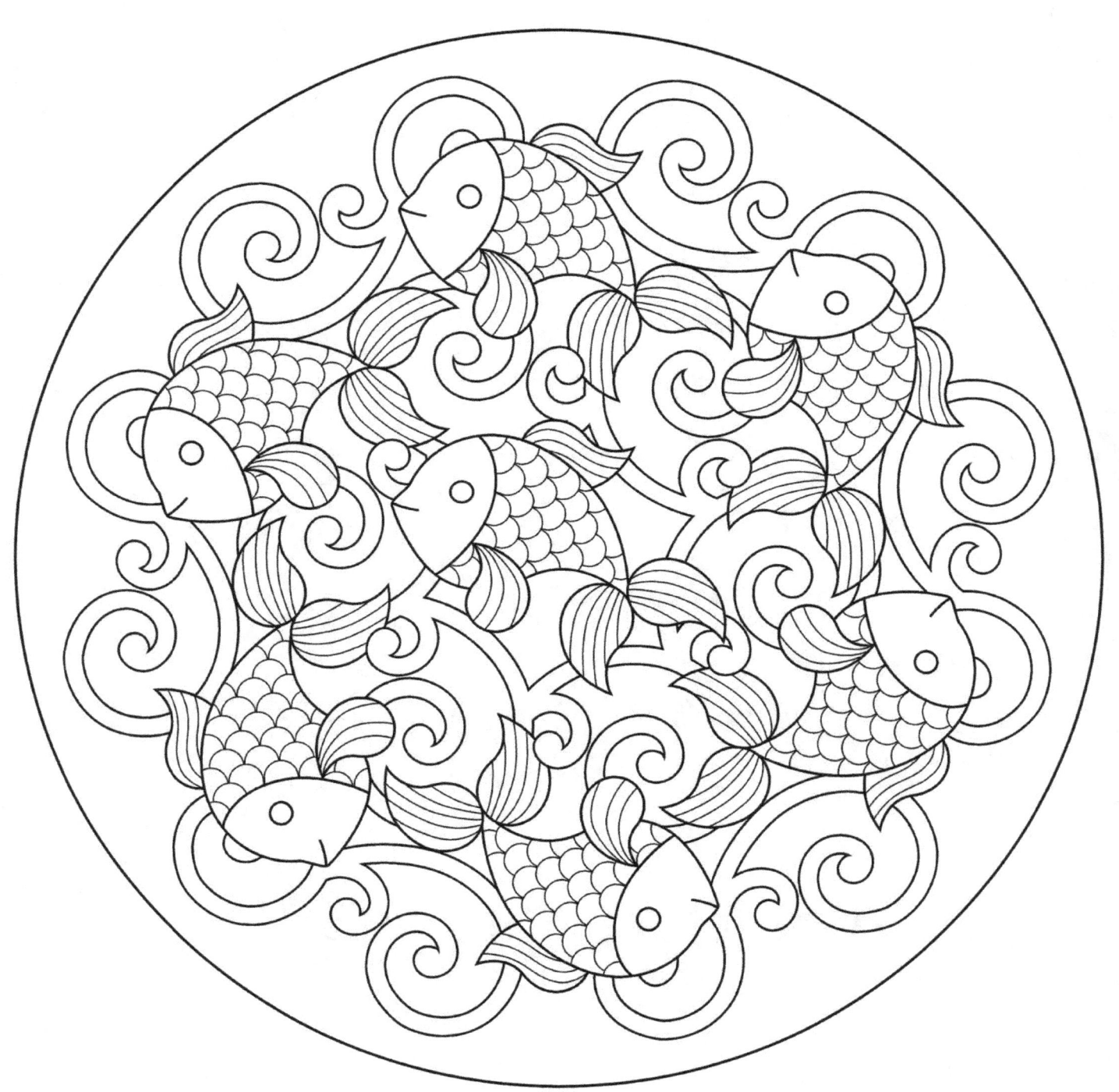

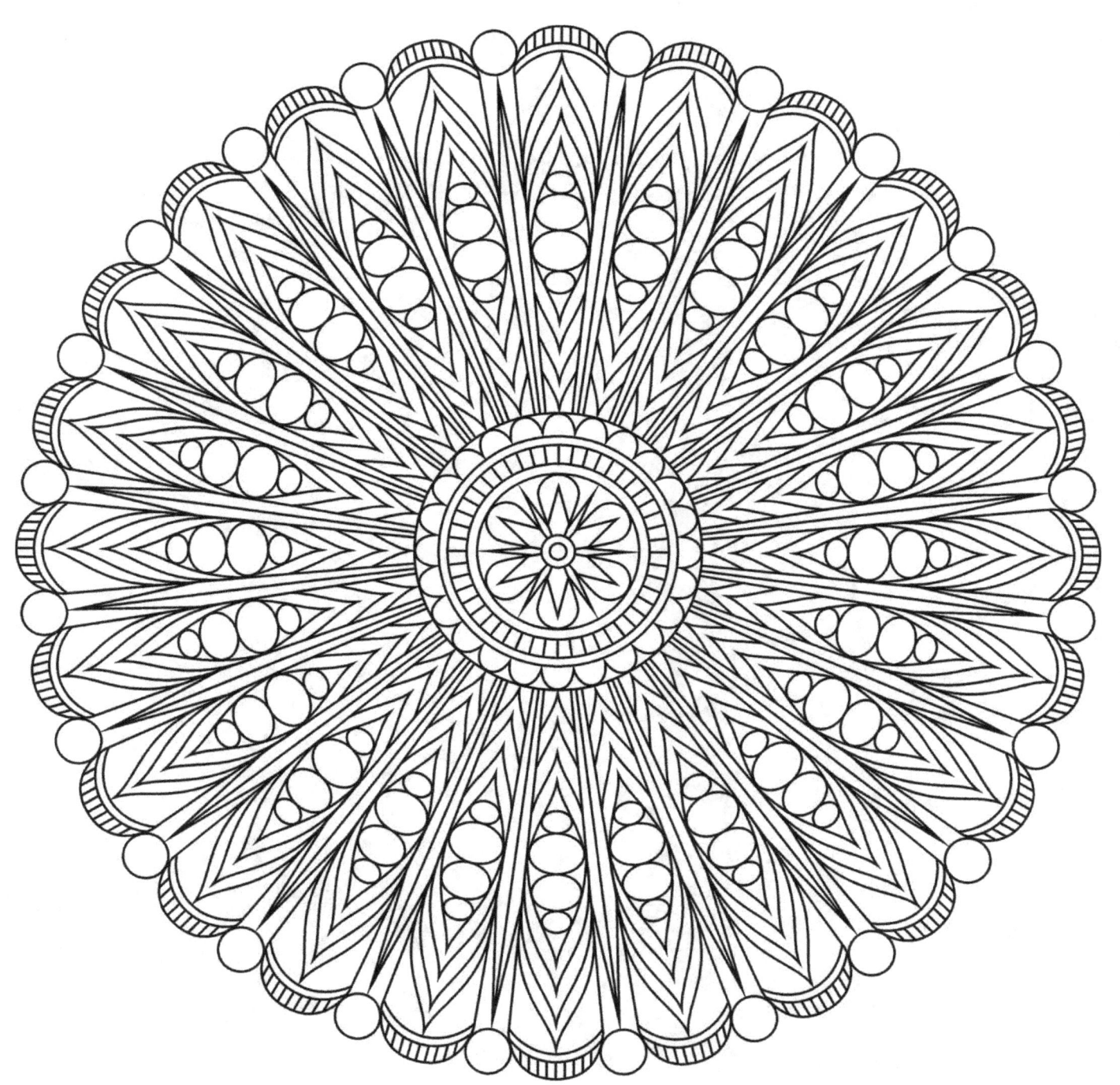

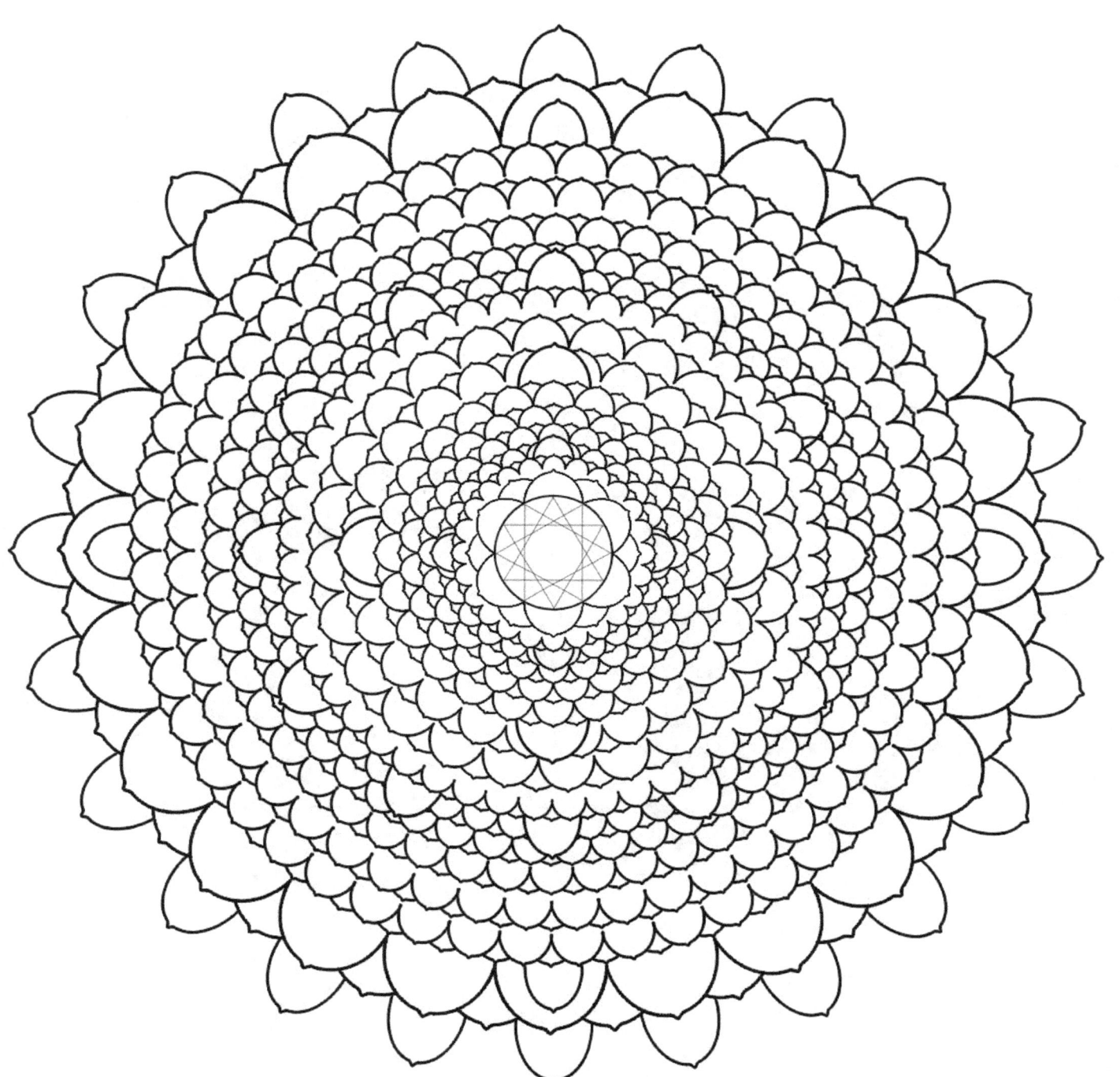

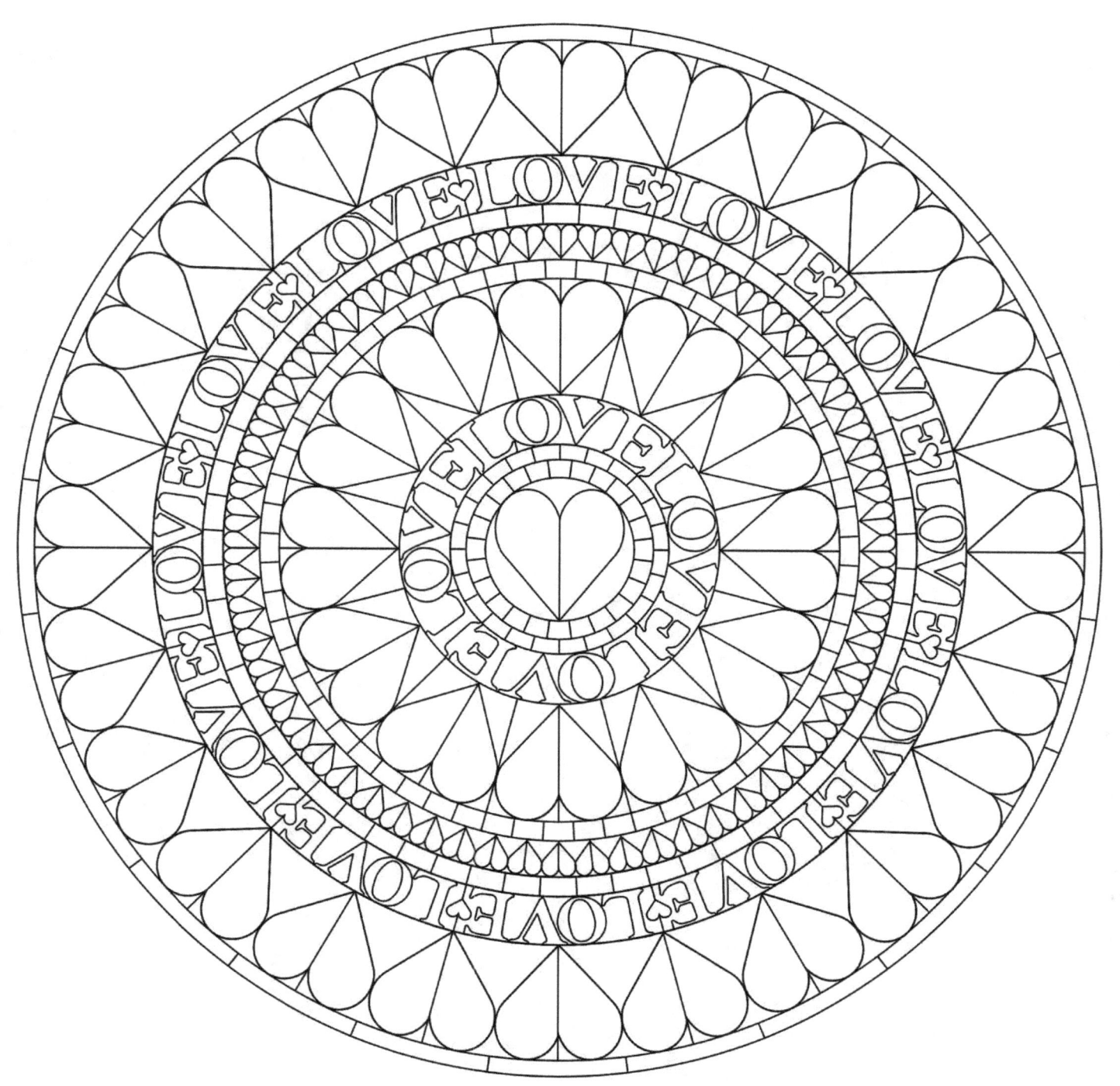

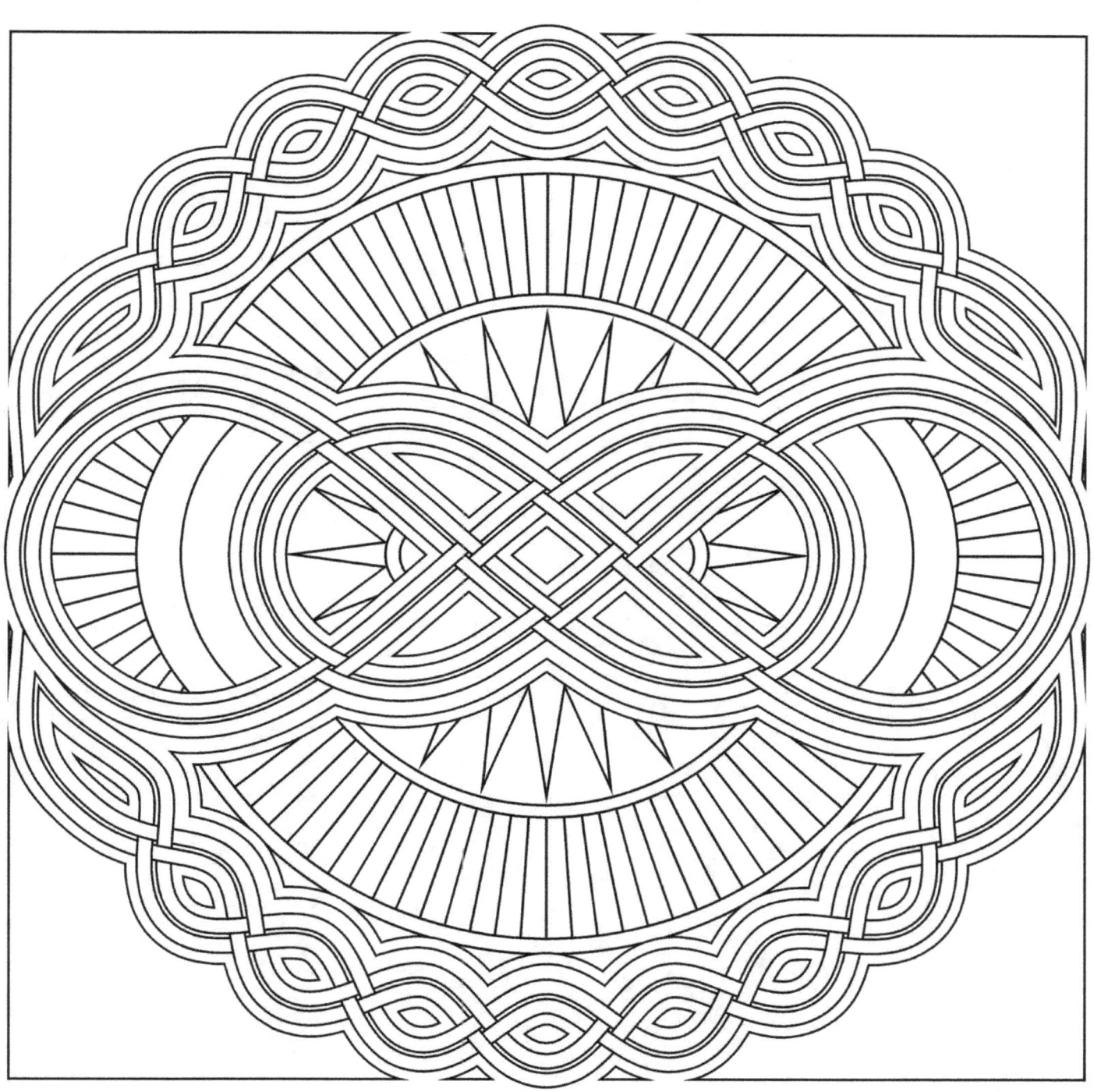

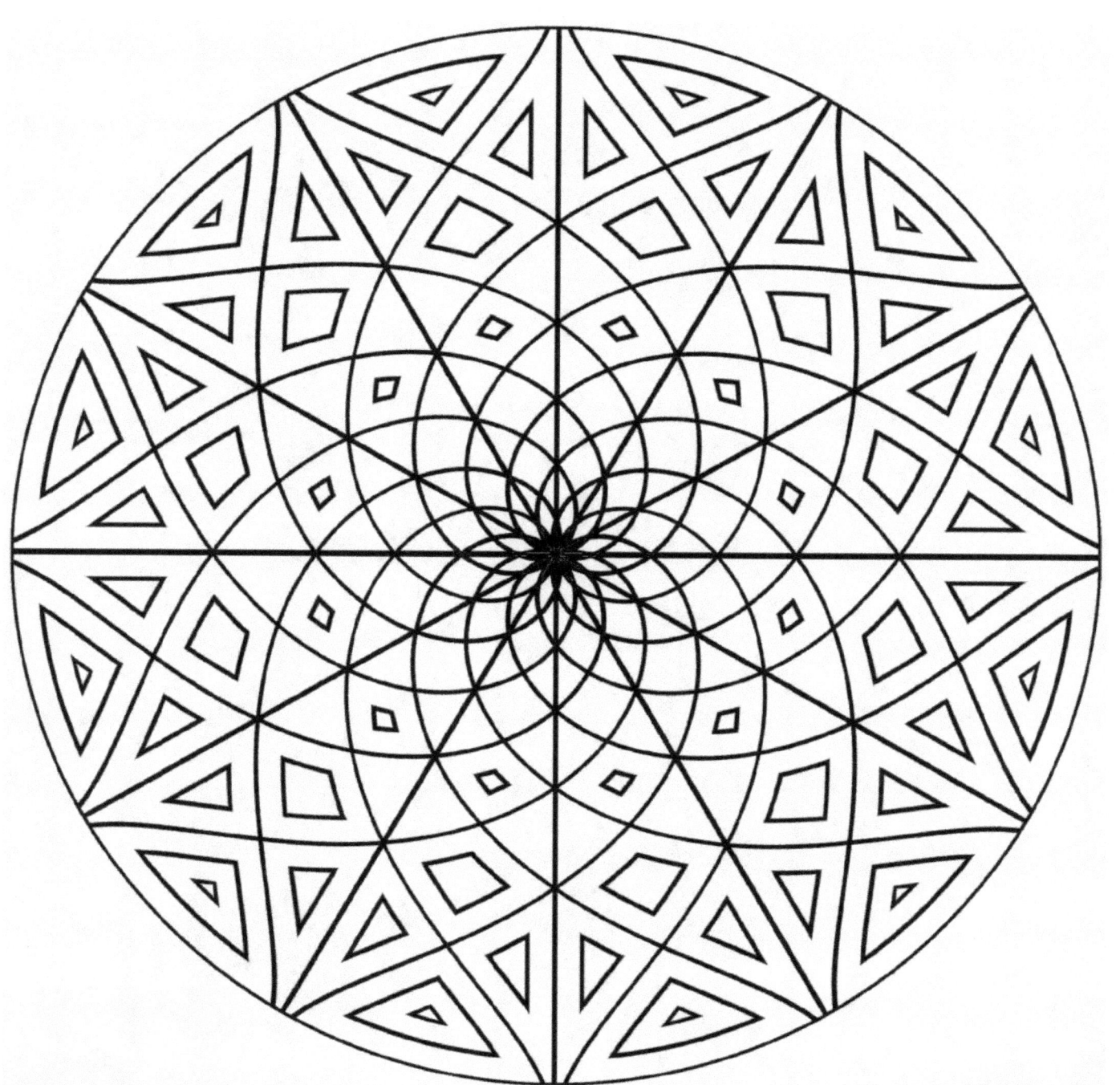

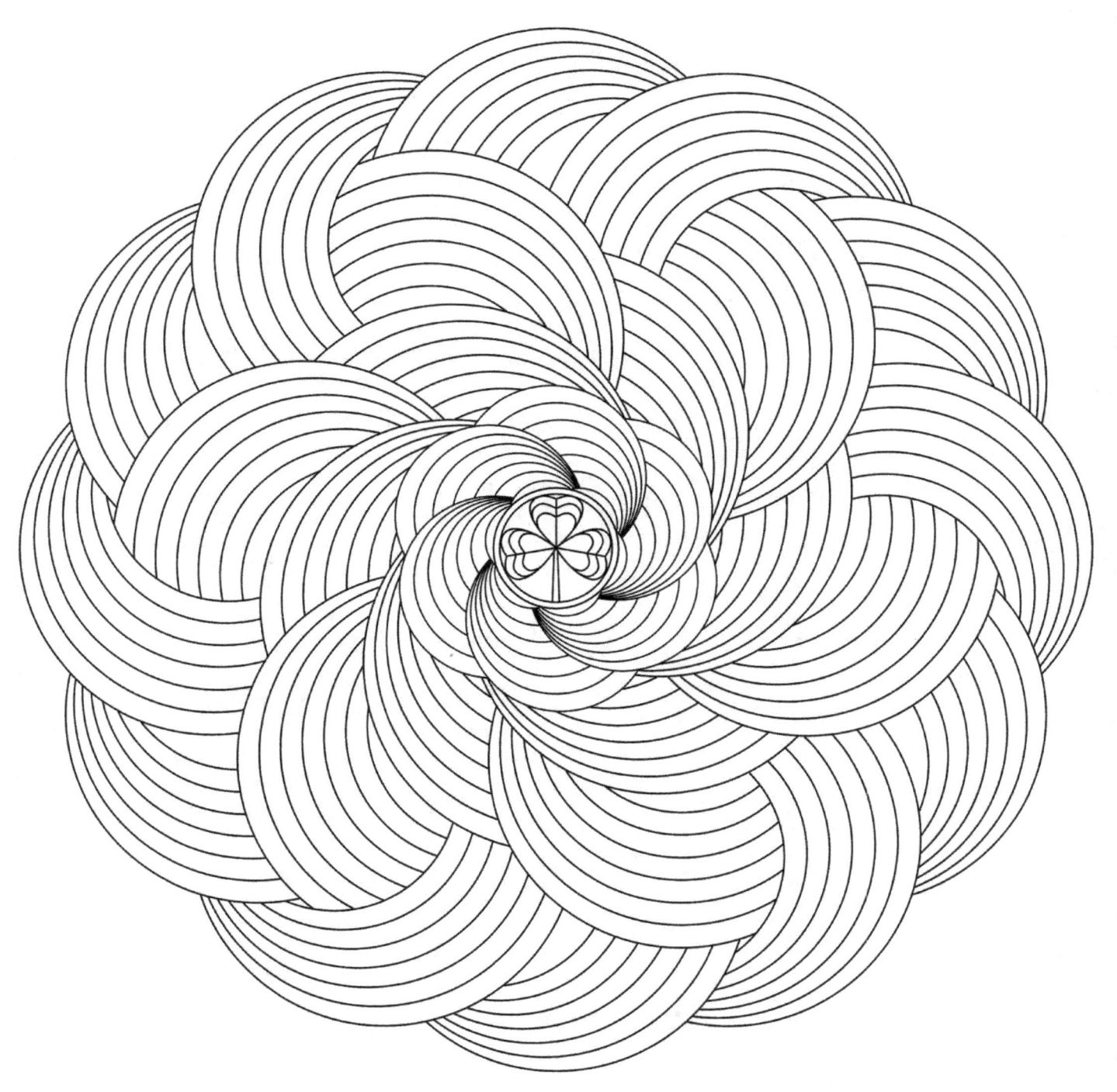

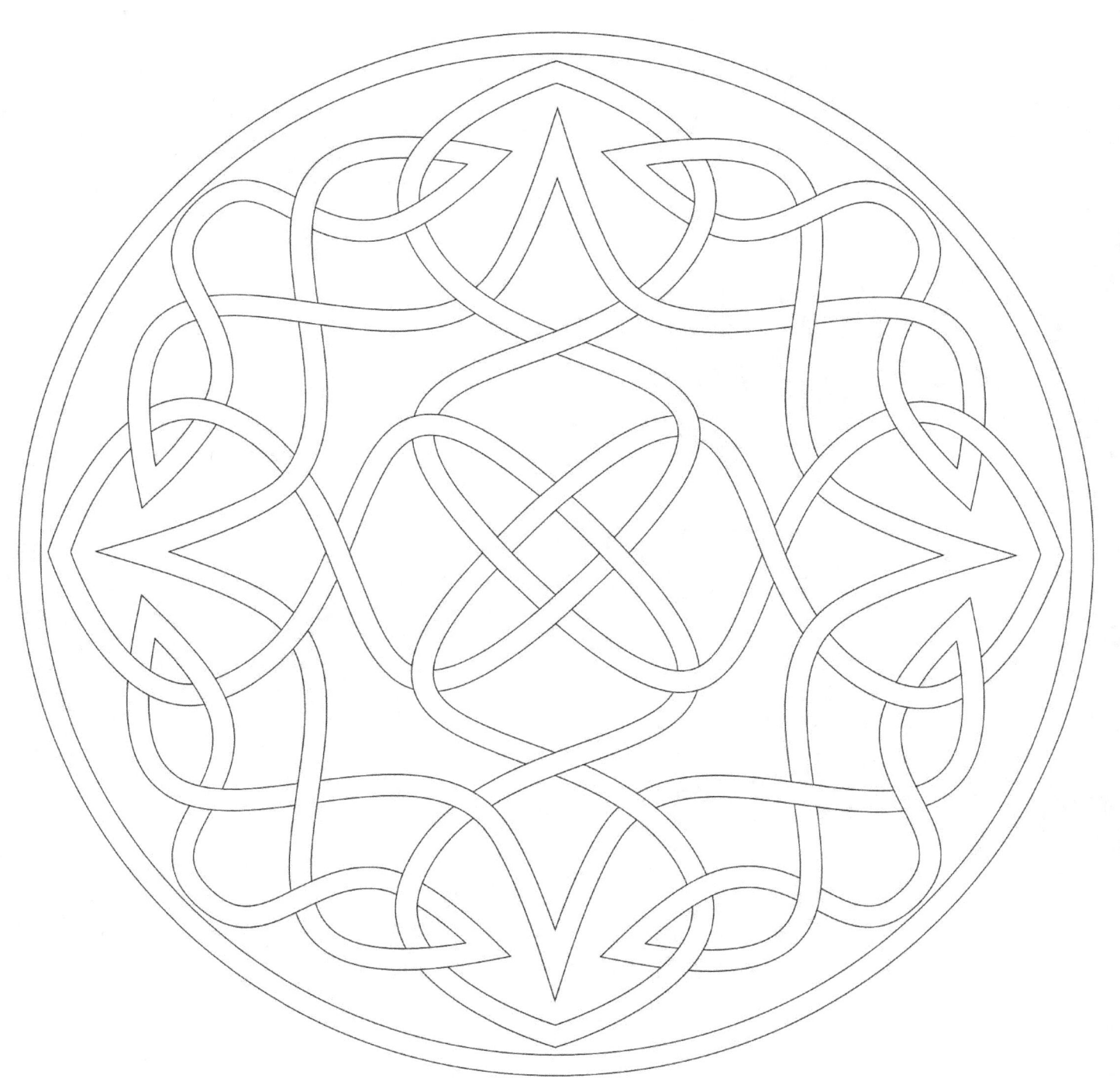

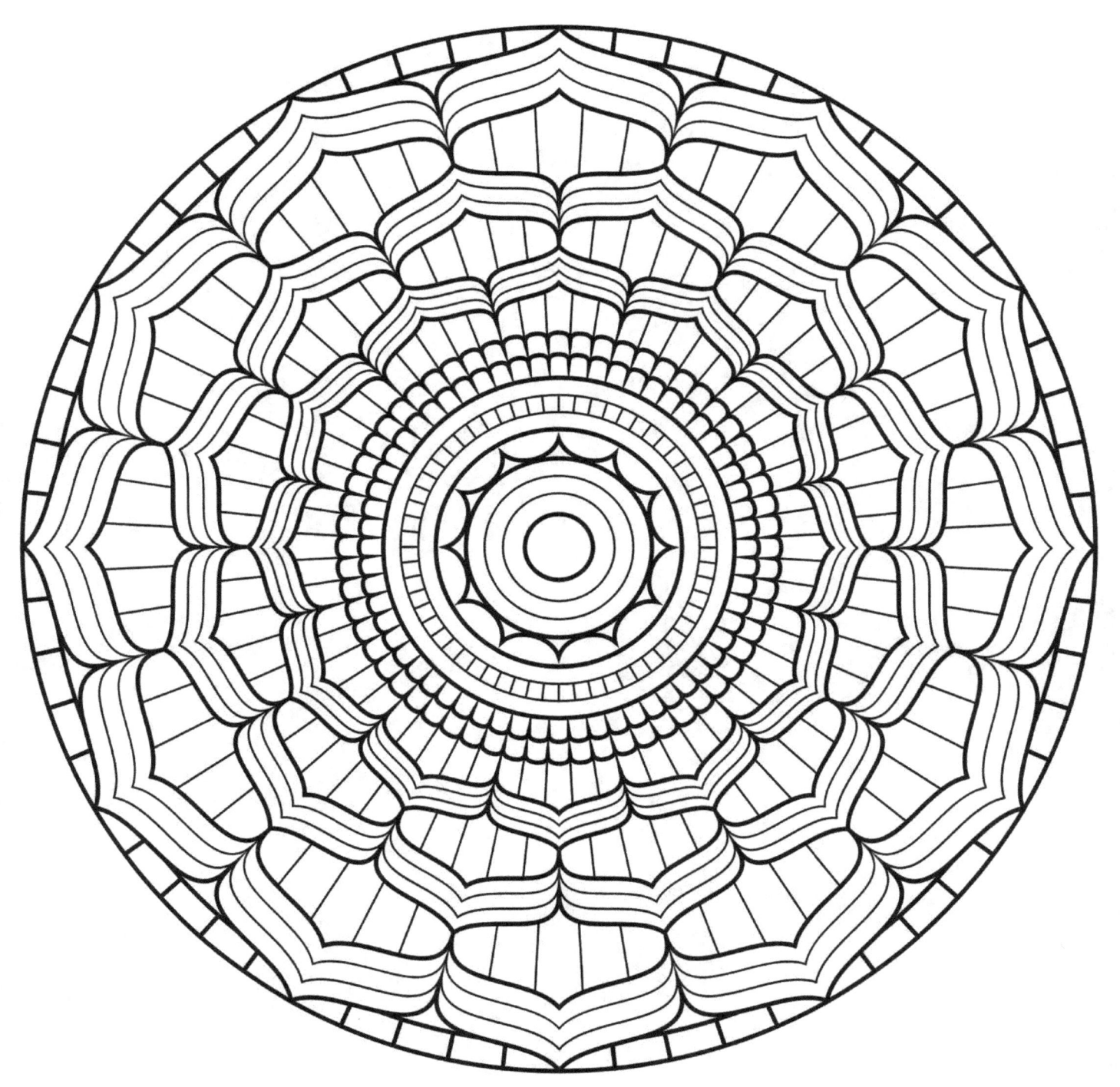

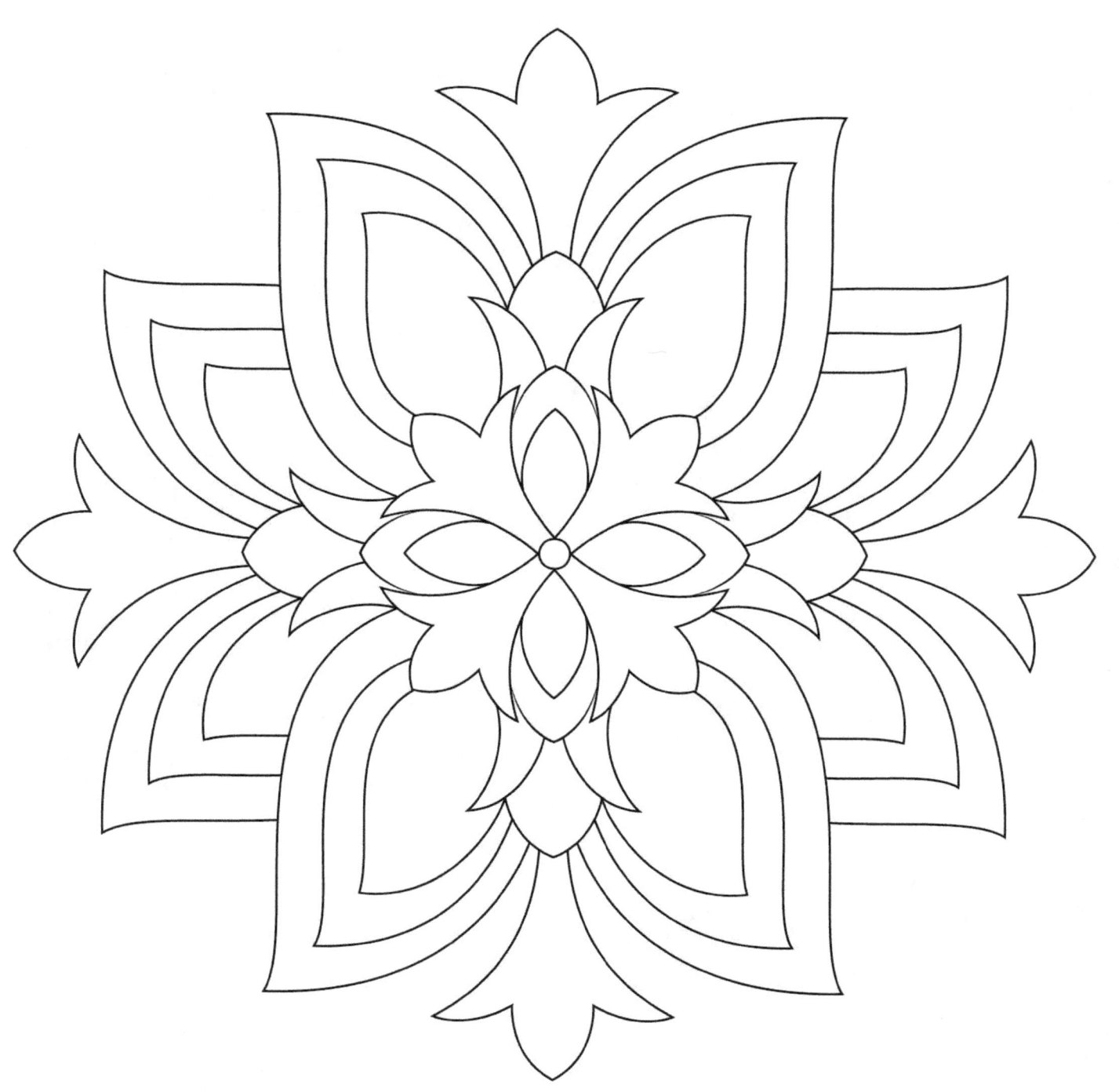

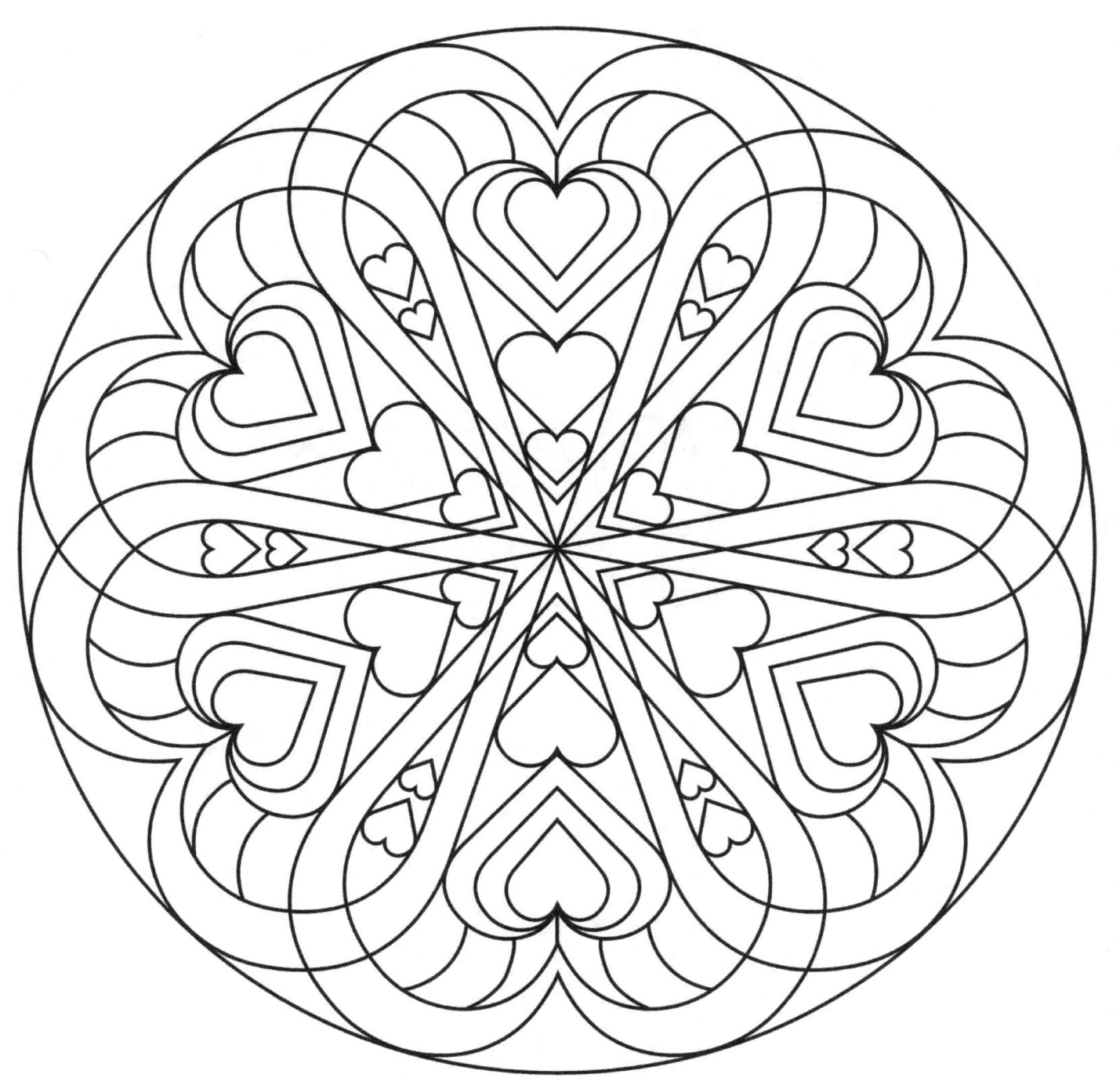

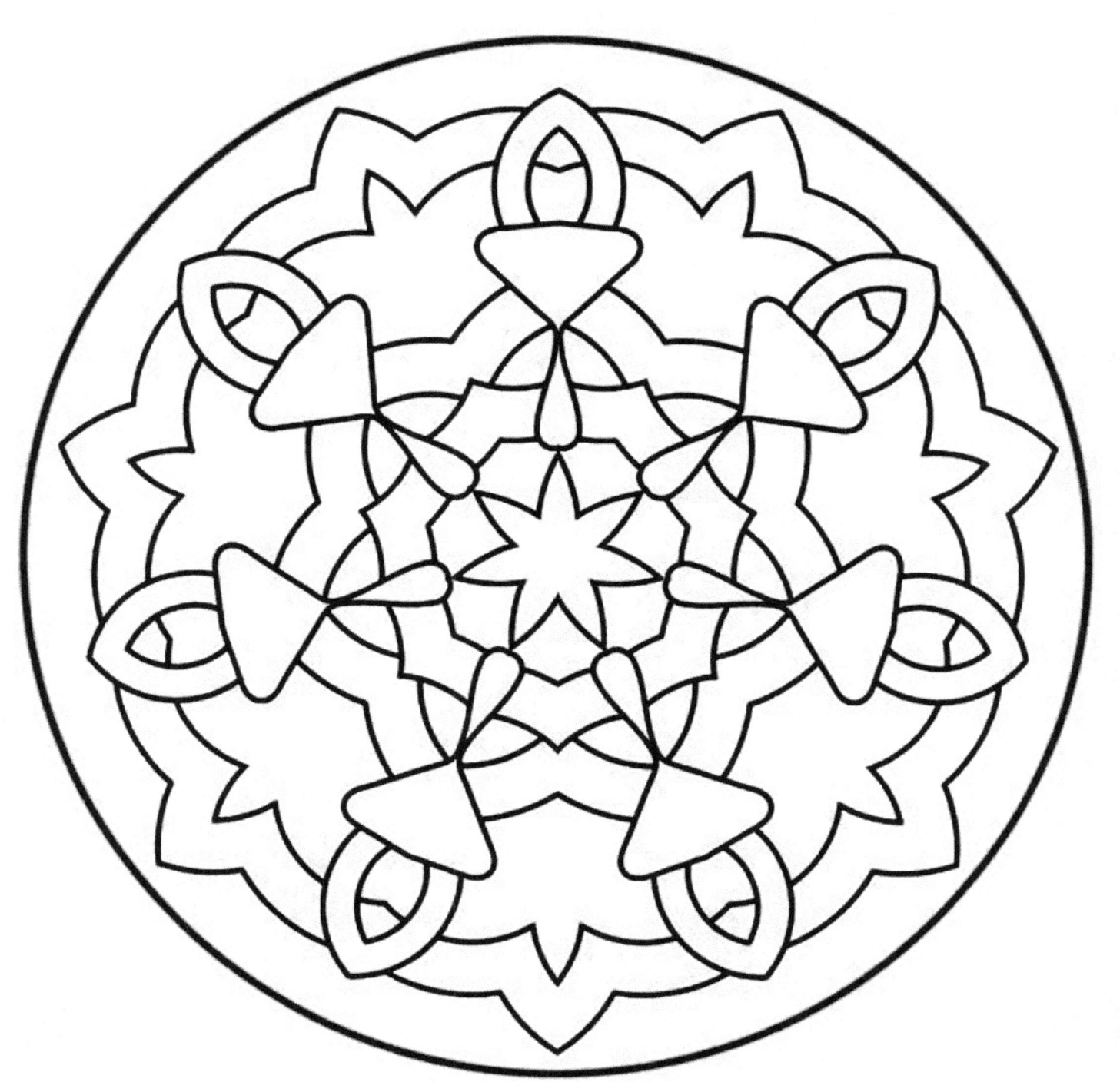

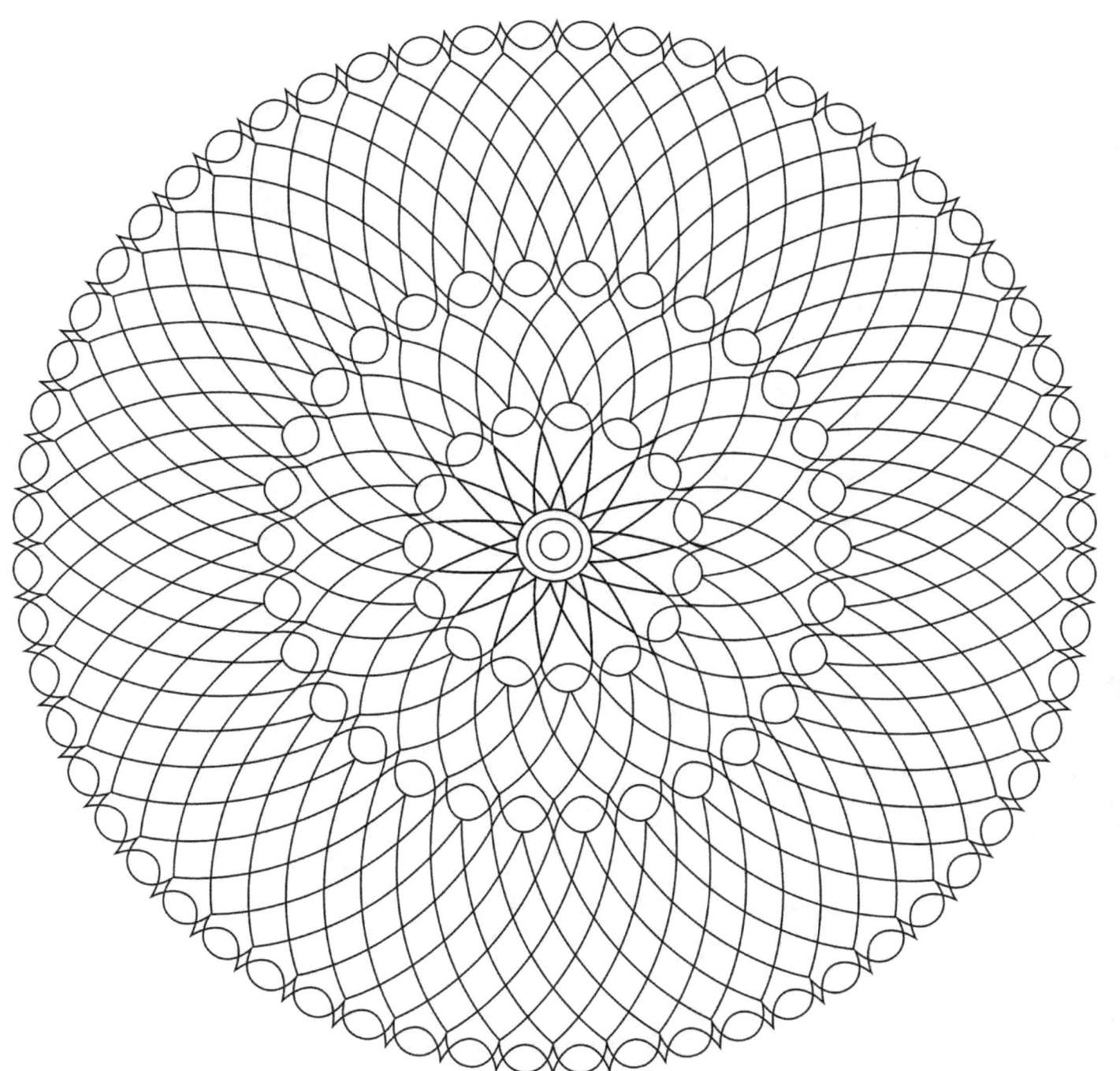

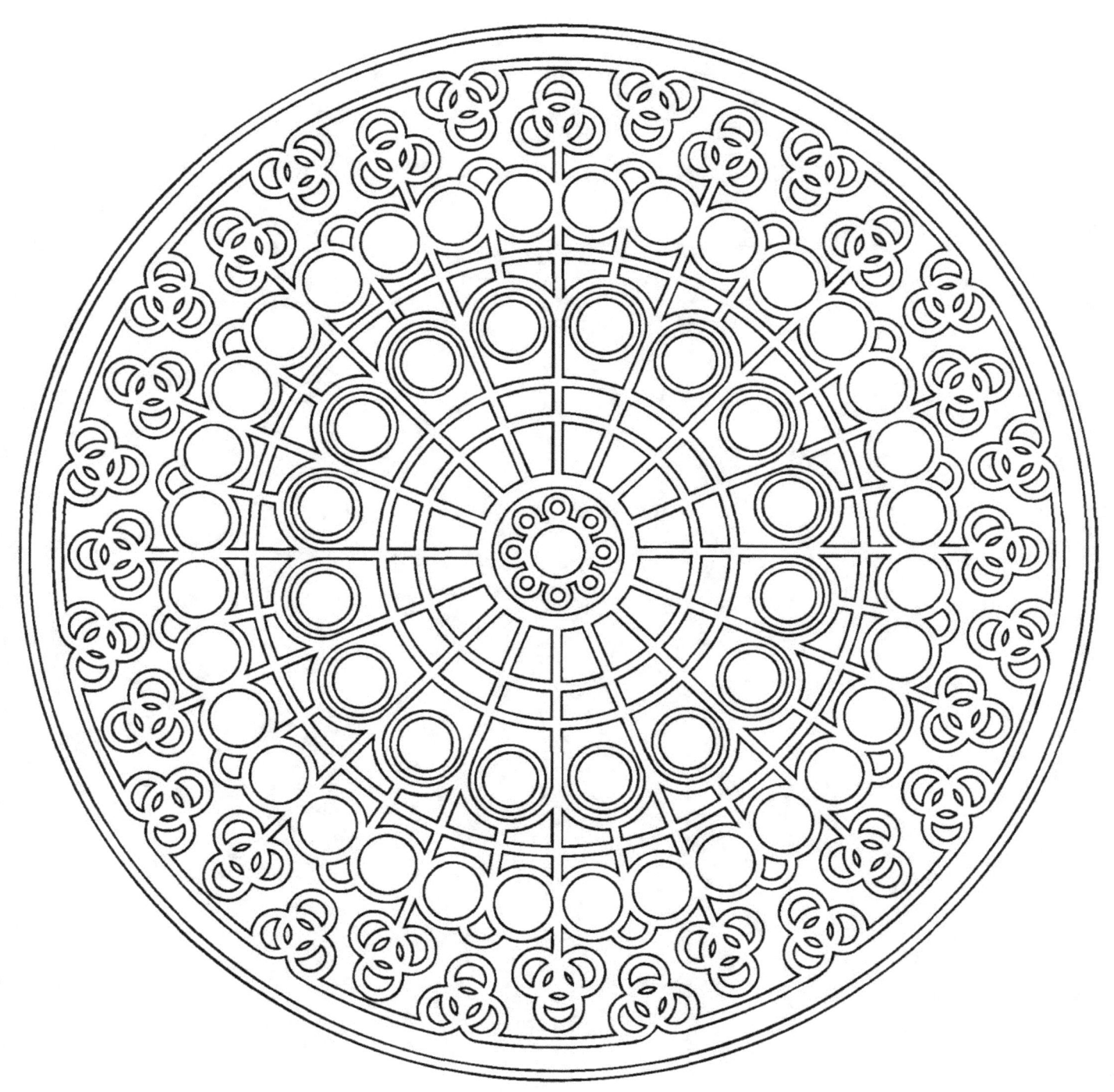

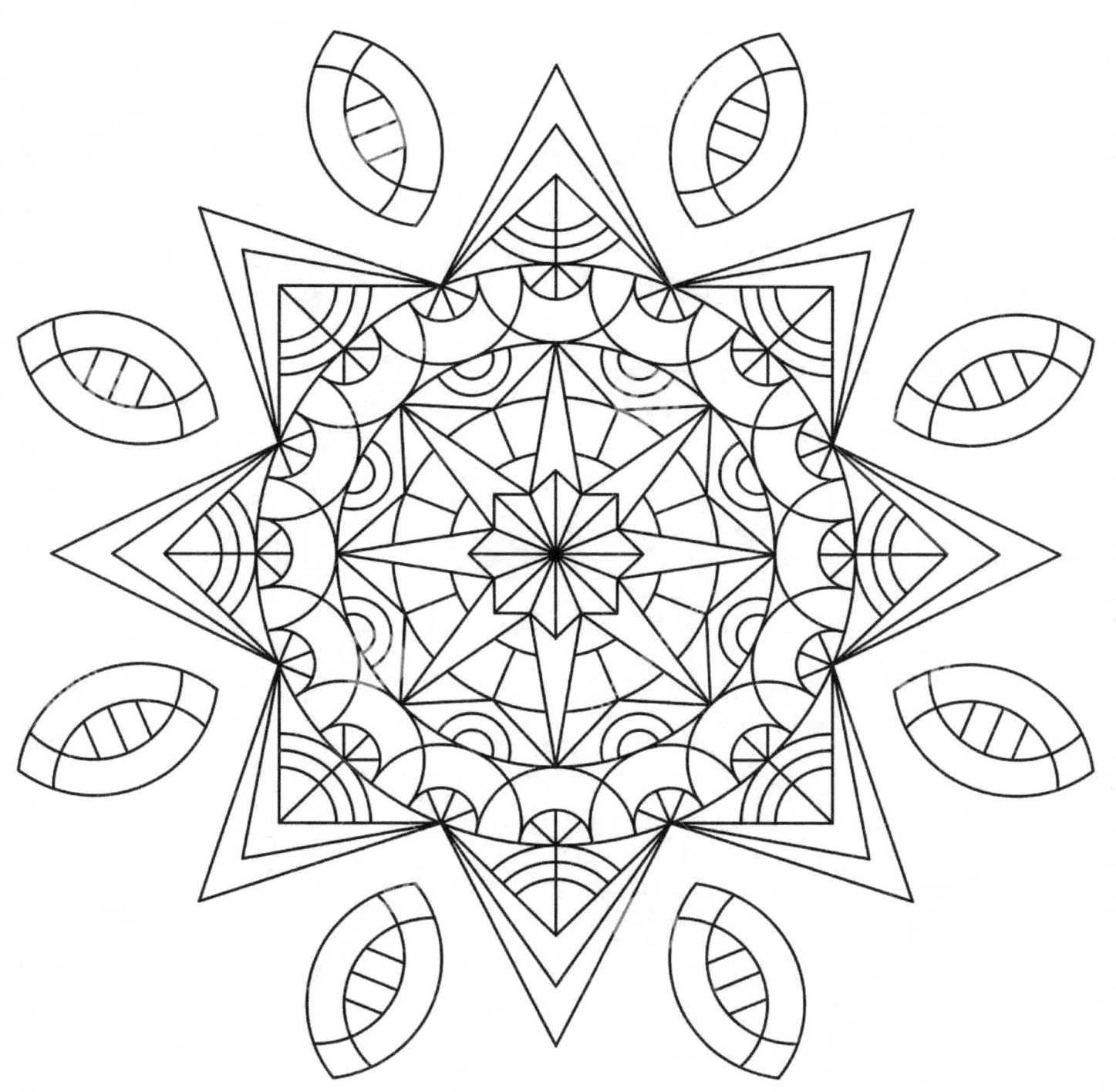

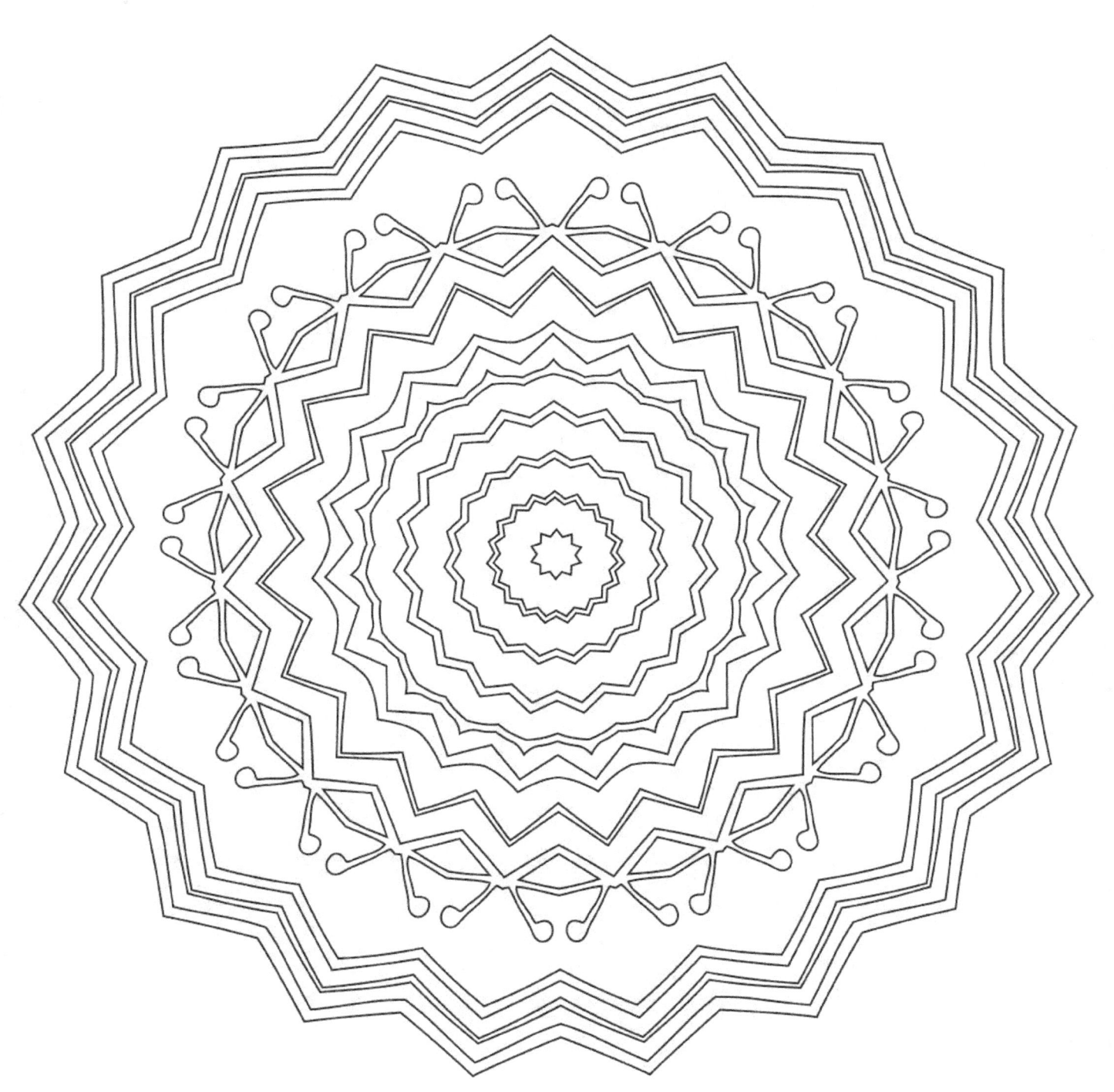

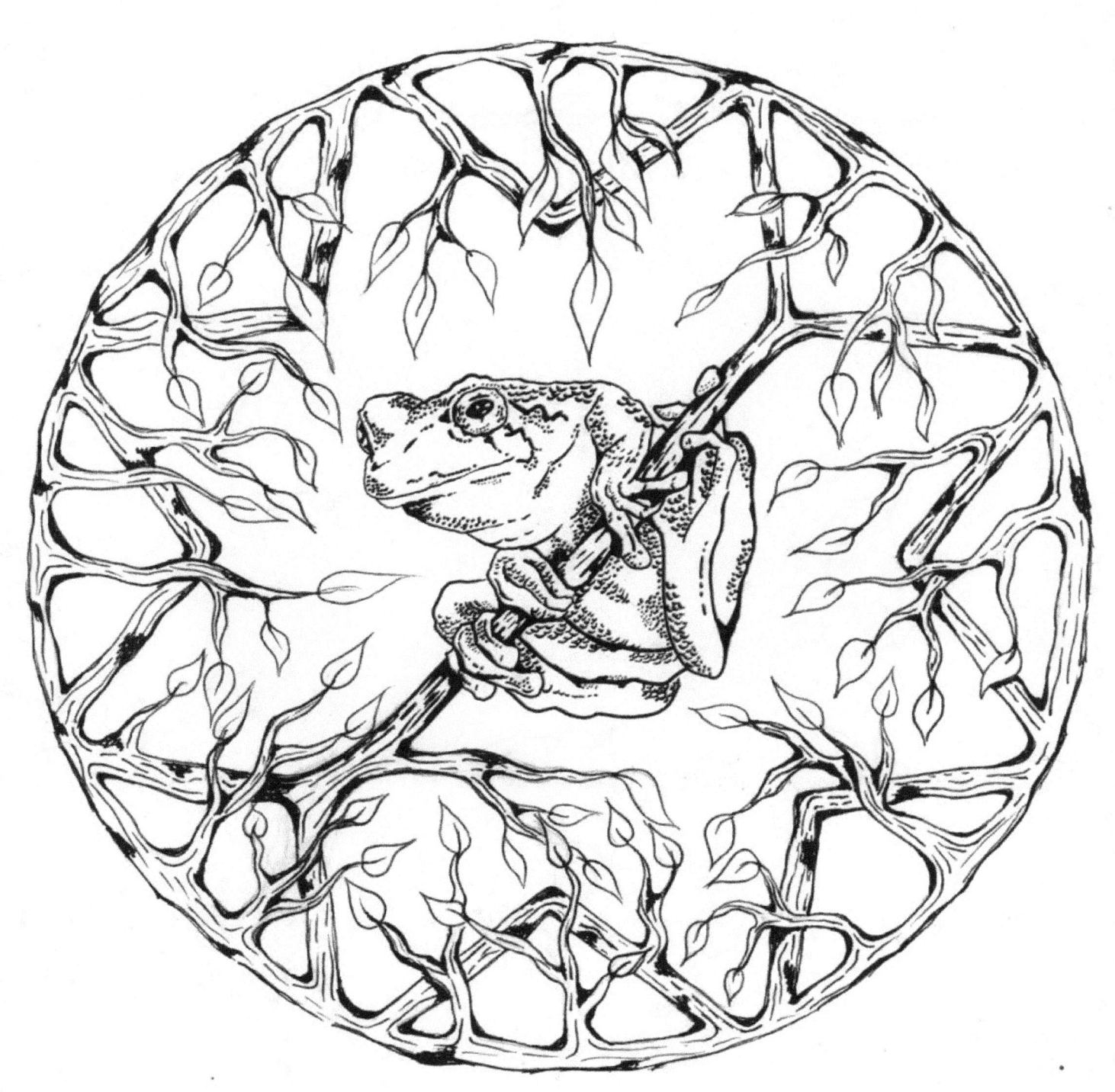

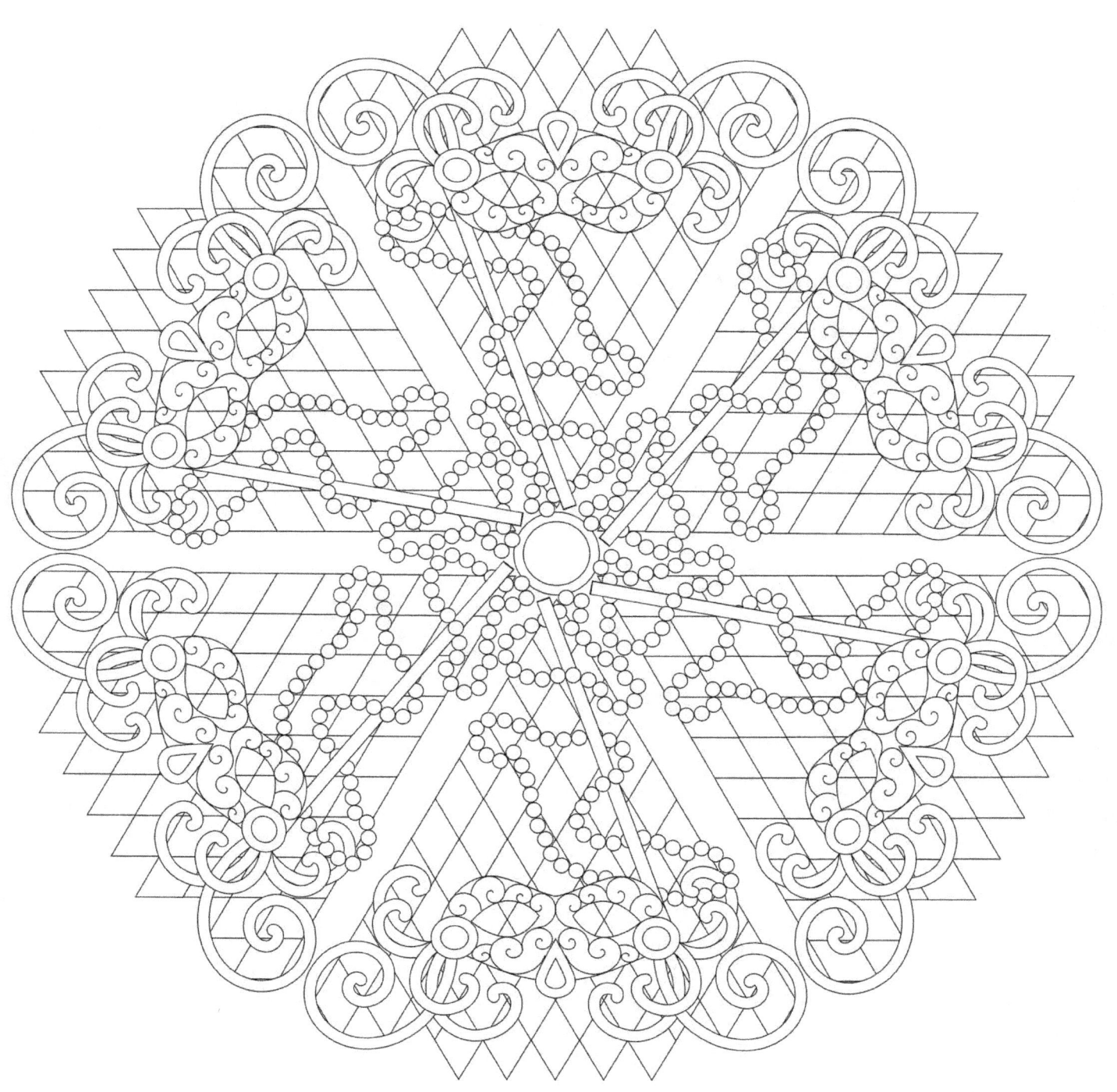

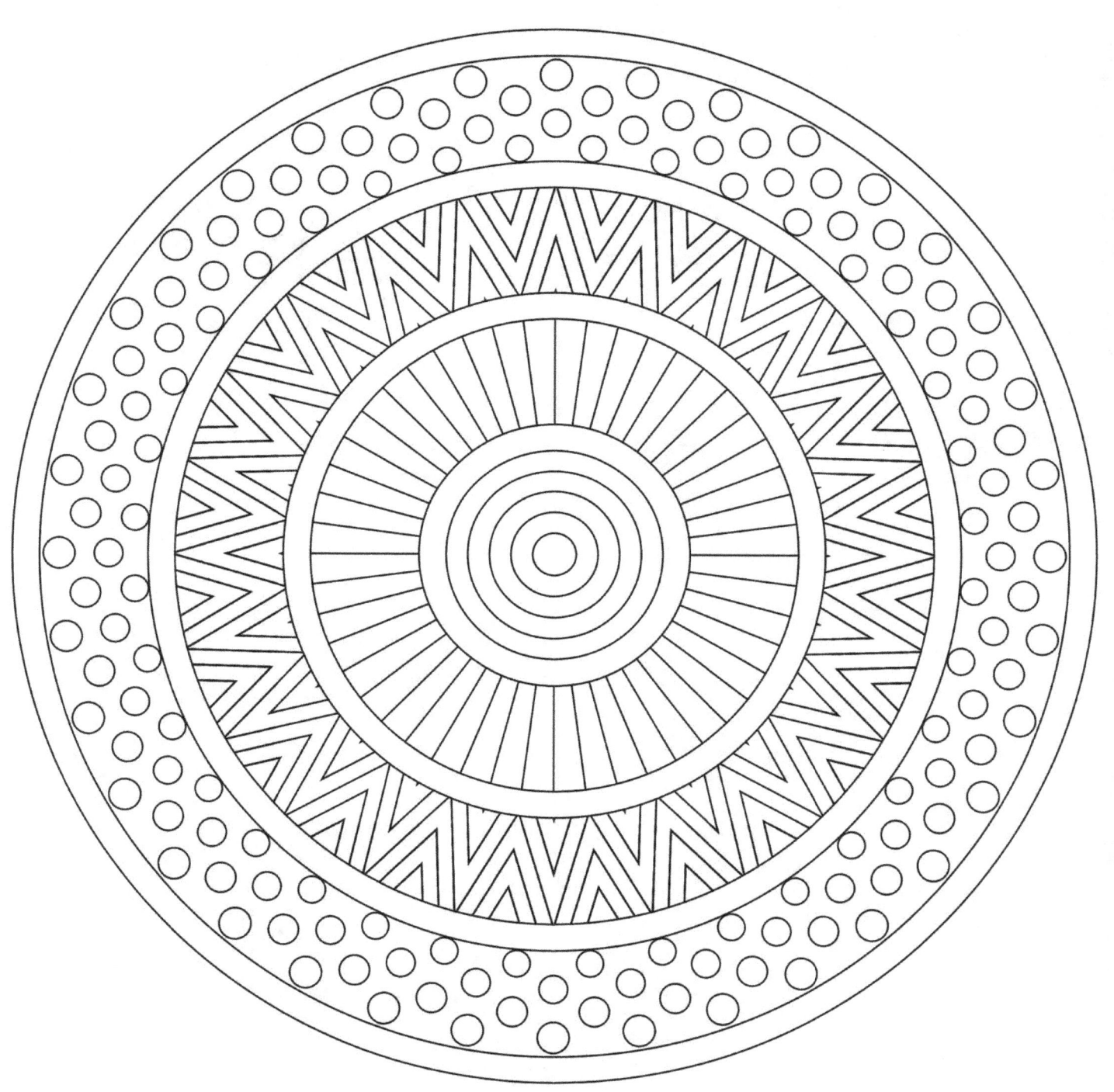

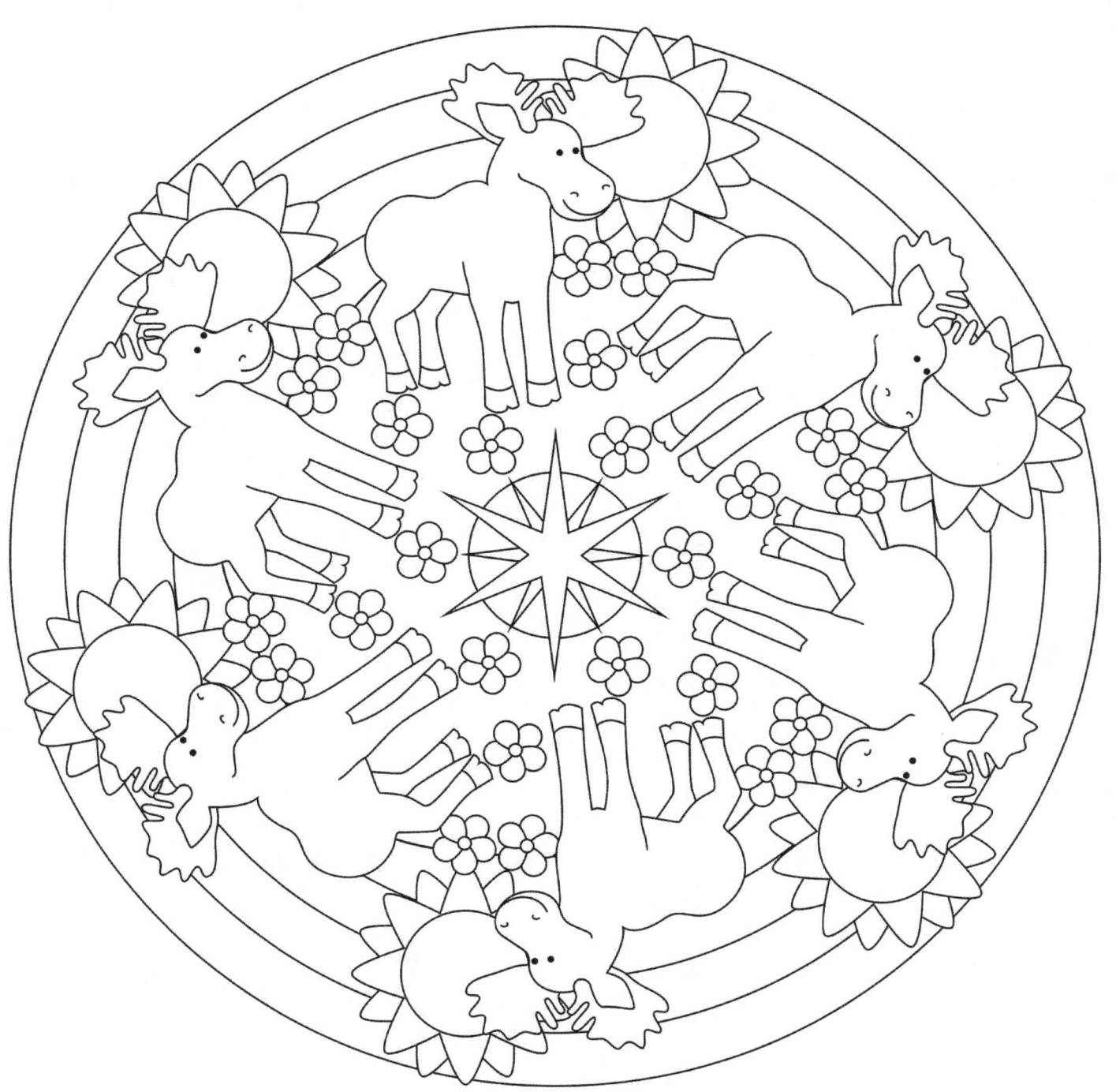